ORDNANCE SURVEY
LEISURE GUIDE

ISLE OF WIGHT

Produced jointly by the Publishing Division of the
Automobile Association and the Ordnance Survey

Cover: *Freshwater Bay looking towards Tennyson Down*
Title page: *luminous sunset from Ryde pier*
Opposite: *thatched cottage at Pound Green, Freshwater*
Introductory page: *rowing boats at Totland Bay*

Editor: Betty Sheldrick

Copy editor: Barry Francis

Art editor: Bob Johnson

Design assistance: Letterbox Design

Editorial contributors: Vicky Basford (The Ancient Island); Anthony Cantwell (Fortifications); Lt Cdr Jim Cheverton (Watching Birds); Jean Cook (Sailing for Pleasure); Oliver Frazer (Nature's Garden Isle); Anthony Goddard (Vineyards); Dr Brian Hinton (Island Celebrities); Jessica Holm (Red Squirrels); Richard Hutchings (Flotsam, Jetsam and Lagan; The Tennyson Circle); Dr Allan Insole (The Making of Wight); Dr Jack Jones (Island History; Carisbrooke Castle); Joanna Jones (Osborne House); Eddie Leal (Walks); Dr Colin Pope (Glanville Fritillary); Ian Rowat (Managing the Landscape); Patricia Sibley (Gazetteer); John Simson (Island in Trust); Tim Slade (Walks); Isle of Wight Tourist Office (Directory)

Picture researcher: Wyn Voysey

Original photography: S & O Mathews

Typeset by Avonset, Midsomer Norton, Bath.
Printed in Great Britain by Chorley & Pickersgill Ltd, Leeds.

Maps extracted from the Ordnance Survey's 1:50 000 Landranger Series, 1:250 000 Routemaster Series and 1:25 000 Outdoor Leisure Map Series, with the permission of Her Majesty's Stationery Office. Crown Copyright reserved.

Additions to the maps by the Cartographic Dept of the Automobile Association and the Ordnance Survey.

Produced by the Publishing Division of the Automobile Association.

Distributed in the United Kingdom by the Ordnance Survey, Southampton, and the Publishing Division of the Automobile Association, Fanum House, Basingstoke, Hampshire RG21 2EA.

AA ISBN 0 86145 666 1 (hardback)
AA ISBN 0 86145 656 4 (softback)
OS ISBN 0 31900 136 9 (hardback)
OS ISBN 0 31900 135 0 (softback)

Published by the Automobile Association and the Ordnance Survey.

AA reference: 55505 (hardback)
AA reference: 55495 (softback)

ISLE OF WIGHT

Contents

Using this Book

The entries in the Gazetteer have been carefully selected although for reasons of space it has not been possible to include every community in the region. A number of small villages are described under the entry for a larger neighbour, and these can be found in the index.

Each entry in the A to Z Gazetteer has the atlas page number on which the place can be found and its National Grid reference included under the heading. An explanation of how to use the National Grid is given on page 80.

Beneath many of the entries in the Gazetteer are listed AA-recommended hotels, restaurants, garages, guesthouses, campsites and self-catering accommodation in the immediate vicinity of the place described.

SELECTION ONLY
For some popular resorts, not all AA-recommended establishments can be included. For full details see current editions of the AA's annual guides and AA *Members' Handbook*.

HOTELS
1-star	Good hotels and inns, generally of small scale and with acceptable facilities and furnishing.
2-star	Hotels offering a higher standard of accommodation, with some private bathrooms/showers; lavatories on all floors; wider choice of food.
3-star	Well-appointed hotels; a good proportion of bedrooms with private bathrooms/showers.
4-star	Exceptionally well-appointed hotels offering a high standard of comfort and service, the majority of bedrooms should have private bathrooms/showers.
5-star	Luxury hotels offering the highest international standards.

Hotels often satisfy *some* of the requirements for higher classifications than that awarded.

Red-star	Red stars denote hotels which are considered to be of outstanding merit within their classification.
Country House Hotel	A hotel where a relaxed informal atmosphere prevails. Some of the facilities may differ from those at urban hotels of the same classification.

RESTAURANTS
1-fork	Modest but good restaurant.
2-fork	Restaurant offering a higher standard of comfort than above.
3-fork	Well-appointed restaurant.
4-fork	Exceptionally well-appointed restaurant.
5-fork	Luxury restaurant.
1-rosette	Hotel or restaurant where the cuisine is considered to be of a higher standard than is expected in an establishment within its classification.
2-rosette	Hotel or restaurant offering very much above average food, irrespective of the classification.
3-rosette	Hotel or restaurant offering outstanding food, irrespective of classification.

GUESTHOUSES
These are different from, but not necessarily inferior to, AA-appointed hotels, and they offer an alternative for those who prefer inexpensive and not too elaborate accommodation. They all provide clean, comfortable accommodation in homely surroundings. Each establishment must usually offer at least six bedrooms, and a general bathroom and a general toilet for every six bedrooms without private facilities.

SELF CATERING
These establishments, which are all inspected on a regular basis, have to meet minimum standards in accommodation, furniture, fixtures and fittings, services and linen.

CAMPSITES
1-pennant	Site licence; 10% of pitches for touring units; site density not more than 30 per acre; 2 separate toilets for each sex per 30 pitches; good quality tapwater; efficient waste disposal; regular cleaning of ablutions block; fire precautions; well-drained ground.
2-pennant	All one-pennant facilities plus: 2 washbasins with hot and cold water for each sex per 30 pitches in separate washrooms; warden available at certain times of the day.
3-pennant	All two-pennant facilities plus: one shower or bath for each sex per 30 pitches, with hot and cold water; electric shaver points and mirrors; all-night lighting of toilet blocks; deep sinks for washing clothes; facilities for buying milk, bread and gas; warden in attendance by day, on call by night.
4-pennant	All three-pennant facilities plus: a higher degree of organisation than one–three-pennant sites; attention to landscaping; reception office; late-arrivals enclosure; first-aid hut; shop; routes to essential facilities lit after dark; play area; bad weather shelter; hard standing for touring vans.
5-pennant	A comprehensive range of services and equipment; careful landscaping; automatic laundry; public telephone; indoor play facilities for children; extra facilities for recreation; warden in attendance 24 hours per day.

Please note that the Island's STD code (0983) should be used only when telephoning from the mainland

ISLE OF WIGHT
Introduction

Only minutes away from the mainland but very far away in atmosphere – the Island, as the locals call it, is not quite like anywhere else. It has all the activities and attractions you could wish for in a holiday, with seaside resorts just as they should be. But it also has miles of orchid-speckled downland, walks along towering chalk cliffs (ideal for birdwatchers), sandy beaches, unspoilt villages . . . and a certain magic all of its own. Written entirely by people who live on the Island, backed by the AA's research expertise and the Ordnance Survey's mapping, this book is for those who know and love the Isle of Wight and for those discovering it for the first time.

The Ancient Island

One of the Island's best-known archaeological monuments
is the 10-ton Longstone near Mottistone,
constructed by New Stone Age farmers

Visitors to the Isle of Wight enjoy – and possibly exaggerate – the features that go with its being an island, but in reality the Island's history has always been bound up with that of southern Britain and particularly with that of the 'Wessex' region. Indeed, for much of its early prehistory, the Wight was still physically attached to the mainland. During the Old Stone Age the area of the Wight would have been accessible to nomadic hunter-gatherers without a sea crossing. Old Stone Age tools have been recovered from gravel deposits and suggest that man was certainly exploiting the resources of the Wight around 80,000 years ago, if not earlier. About 10,000 years ago the sea level around the British coast began to rise as the great ice sheets of the last Ice Age melted. As the sea level rose, the estuary of the River Solent was gradually inundated until eventually, between 8,000 and 6,000 years ago, the Isle of Wight became separated from the mainland. During the rise in sea level the river valleys of the Medina, the eastern and western Yar and other inlets along the northern coast of the Island were flooded. Middle Stone Age 'camp sites' with hearths and flint tools have been found buried under later deposits of estuarine silt and clay in these drowned river valleys. On the south-western side of the Island, coastal erosion has exposed the former river valley of the western Yar in the cliff face, and the hearths of further Middle Stone Age 'camp sites' have been observed in the cliff, together with plant remains.

The prehistoric past

During the Ice Ages, conditions were too cold for the establishment of woodland. As temperatures rose after the end of the last Ice Age, the vegetation changed from low-growing plants to birch scrub, succeeded by pine and hazel and finally by thick deciduous woodland covering much of the Island. Dr Robert Scaife, who has carried out extensive pollen analysis on the Isle of Wight, has been able to establish the changing pattern of the Island's woodland by studying pollen grains preserved in peat deposits. The first evidence of substantial disturbance by man seems to have occurred about 5,000 years ago, when there is local evidence of a dramatic decline in the number of elm trees. This decline occurs throughout Britain at this time and is associated with the introduction of animal husbandry and cereal cultivation by New Stone Age people. Pollen samples from peat formed at this time on the Isle of Wight have given evidence of shifting cultivation taking place in temporary forest clearances, and it is apparent that the Chalklands and Greensand ridges were not extensively cleared during the New Stone Age.

The Longstone, near Mottistone, is a free-standing upright stone of local Greensand beside which lies another large stone. Behind these stones is a low mound, the remains of a long barrow or burial mound. The mound has been partially excavated but no burials were found.

No houses of New Stone Age date have been found on the Isle of Wight but New Stone Age pottery has been found beneath round barrow cemeteries dating from the Bronze Age, and this suggests that the New Stone Age farmers may have occupied the same sites as their Bronze Age successors. The Afton Down long barrow – the only other burial mound of New Stone Age date besides the Longstone – is surrounded by Bronze Age barrows and provides additional evidence for

Afton Down long barrow is one of the well preserved burial mounds that dates back to the New Stone Age

continuity of settlement. There is also evidence for New Stone Age settlement of the three main river valleys. At Gatcombe, pollen remains and associated flint tools provide evidence for clearance of the valley side, occupation and surrounding arable cultivation of the Greensand soils.

An enigmatic mound on Tennyson Down has been thought to be of New Stone Age date. Dr David Tomalin, the County Archaeological Officer, has suggested that it may have been a mortuary enclosure – a site where the bodies of the dead were left exposed until the flesh had rotted away. The bones would then be collected up for burial in a long barrow. Another probable mortuary house has now been located beneath a Bronze Age burial mound on Gallibury Down, recently excavated by the Isle of Wight Archaeological Committee.

The Island has over 240 Bronze Age burial mounds, known as round barrows. Nearly all of these barrows are on the chalk downs. The downland burial sites may have been associated with springline settlement at the foot of the downs. Some of the barrows have now been completely ploughed away and others are covered with trees. The best-preserved round barrows are on the unploughed chalk grassland of the West Wight. A walk along part of the 'Tennyson Trail' from the Mottistone Down car park offers the best introduction to the Isle of Wight Bronze Age. The trail follows the route of a prehistoric trackway and there are well-preserved groups of barrows on Mottistone Down, Brook Down, East Afton Down and Afton Down. The chalk grassland on which these barrow groups are situated dates back to the Bronze Age. Before this time the chalk downs would have been covered in trees except for the most exposed coastal areas, but there is pollen evidence for the extensive clearance of chalklands during the Bronze Age.

Numerous hill-forts are a feature of the Iron Age in mainland 'Wessex'. On the Isle of Wight only one hill-fort is known, on Chillerton Down, and

this was probably never completed. This lack of hill-forts is perhaps not surprising in view of the Island's small size. However, it is possibly more puzzling that the many small farmstead enclosures of Iron Age date which are known on the mainland have not been recorded in large numbers on the Isle of Wight. An earthwork enclosure at Castle Hill, near Mottistone, is thought to belong to the Iron Age, and at Knighton, near Newchurch, an Iron Age enclosure which had been ploughed flat was discovered and excavated some years ago. Gradually, Isle of Wight archaeologists are locating more ploughed enclosures and other sites from the study of aerial photographs. Fieldwork earlier this century located remains of a very specialised Iron Age community in the Undercliff. These remains consisted of middens or rubbish pits close to the shore, suggesting a community living mainly from the resources of the sea and seashore.

The Island of Vectis

In the spring of AD43 the troops of the Roman emperor Claudius landed on the Kent coast with the object of conquering Britain. Conquest of the south and west was entrusted to the future emperor Vespasian. The 2nd-century writer Suetonius tells us that Vespasian 'reduced to subjection . . . the island of Vectis very near to Britannia'. This comment implies that the Island was taken by force, but there is no evidence of an armed struggle. Possibly, the islanders surrendered without a fight and were spared a military occupation. However, Dr David Tomalin has recently hinted at a possible early military presence on the evidence of bronze finds from beneath the later villas of Brading and Newport.

Whatever the circumstances of the Island's surrender to Vespasian, it does not appear to have interfered greatly with the local way of life. Villas at Newport, Brading and possibly at Combley appear to have been built on or near the site of previous late Iron Age settlements. These three villas and others at Rock, Clatterford and Carisbrooke are closely associated with the Island's central range of chalk downs. Large flocks of sheep belonging to the villa owners may have been kept on the downs, although on Brading Down – close to the Roman villa – a fine series of ancient fields provides evidence for arable farming on the chalk. The villas of Vectis, like those of mainland Britian, were essentially Romanised farmsteads belonging to wealthy British landowners. Some of these villa proprietors were probably the descendants of Iron Age tribal leaders.

No towns or metalled roads are known to have existed in Roman Wight, which was essentially a rural community. However, indications such as the position of Newport and Brading villas close to natural harbours suggest that trade was important. Large quantities of Roman pottery found in shallow water off Yarmouth indicate that a coastal trading settlement may have existed close by.

Newport and Brading villas are open to the public and both are worth visiting as they complement each other. Newport Villa possesses a fine example of a centrally-heated bath suite, and the reconstruction of a Roman kitchen.

Brading Villa possesses nationally famous mosaic pavements which abound in literary and mythological scenes and are highly important to our understanding of late Romano-British culture.

The Dark Ages

With the collapse of the 'market economy' in Roman Britain at the end of the 4th century, the whole basis of the villa system was destroyed. Villas such as Brading, which had been at their most prosperous earlier in the century, were now abandoned.

We know that occupation of all the Island villas had ceased by the early 5th century. However, the British inhabitants of Wight must have continued to live on the Island long after the breakdown of the villa system, for the Anglo-Saxon Chronicle claims that in AD530 the Anglo-Saxon chieftains Cerdic and Cynric 'obtained the possession of the Isle of Wight and slew many men at Wihtgarabyrig'. The site of this alleged massacre may have been at Carisbrooke Castle but this is highly debatable and there is no archaeological evidence for such a slaughter. What evidence there is suggests a gradual influx of Anglo-Saxon colonists to the Isle of Wight, rather than a rapid military operation.

Top left: one of the many 'almost mint' gold coins discovered on the Island. Above: the head of Medusa, superbly depicted in a Roman mosaic at Brading Villa. Top right: a beautifully preserved Anglo-Saxon brooch. Right: reconstruction of a Roman kitchen area at Newport Villa

On the chalk downs of Bowcombe and Chessell, two major Anglo-Saxon cemeteries were discovered and excavated in the last century. The finds from these cemeteries illustrate graphically the nature of pagan Anglo-Saxon society on the Isle of Wight. The distinctive character of the grave goods connects them with the prosperous culture of the Anglo-Saxon kingdom of Kent and beyond, to the Franks of northern France. Of outstanding importance is the collection of rich and exotic material from the large burial ground at Chessell Down, which was acquired by the British Museum in 1867 and 1869. A detailed study of the Chessell grave goods carried out by Dr Christopher Arnold, an authority on Anglo-Saxon burial sites, provides evidence of the importation of luxury goods and the export of locally manufactured products. From his study of Chessell, Bowcombe and other Anglo-Saxon cemeteries on the Isle of Wight, Dr Arnold has concluded that the earliest Anglo-Saxon occupation of the Island may date from as early as the late 5th century.

The latest objects in the Isle of Wight cemeteries date to the end of the 6th century. There is no archaeological evidence for the 7th century, although the Anglo-Saxon Chronicle mentions the Isle of Wight in 661 and 686. It appears that the settlers on the Isle of Wight were independent from the mainland kingdom of the West Saxons until the late 7th century. Indeed, the 8th-century writer Bede attributes the settlement of the Isle of Wight to a distinct tribe called the Jutes, who also settled in Kent and southern Hampshire. Bede claims that the Isle of Wight accepted Christianity 'last of all the provinces of Britain'. He dates this conversion to 686, after Caedwalla, the king of the West Saxons, had laid waste the Island 'which was still entirely devoted to idolatry'.

Excavations in nearby Hampshire have discovered that early Anglo-Saxon settlements such as Chalton were located high on the chalk downs, some distance from the later medieval settlement in the valley. It is tempting to suppose that there may be an early settlement close to the pagan cemetery on Bowcombe Down – a predecessor of the later settlement at Carisbrooke. What, then, are the origins of the existing Island villages? It has been suggested that the West Saxons established 'planned villages' following their victory over the Jutish inhabitants of the Island in 686. However, the traditional view that most English villages originated in the early to mid-Saxon period is now being challenged by landscape historians. Villages, as such, may not have existed before the 11th century or later.

Fieldwork, excavation and the detailed study of finds are all contributing to our understanding of the Island's past. It is sad that no museum exists where visitors can view the Island's splendid archaelogical collection; however, moves are afoot to provide a museum in Newport within the next few years. Only then can the recent discoveries about the Island's archaeology and the heritage of finds from the past be fully appreciated.

Vicky Basford is the author of The Vectis Report, *a survey of Island archaeology and was formerly on the staff of the County Council Archaeological Unit.*

Island History

'Enough and to spare' might have been the Island's motto, and signs of this fruitfulness may be found at almost any period. The Danish raiders in the early years of the 11th century liked nothing better than to make their winter camp in the Island where, clearly, there was good eating. Edward I, on campaign in Scotland at the beginning of the 14th century, ordered at least two shiploads of corn from the Island (little of it got through: one ship was wrecked, and the other arrived storm-tossed and with a damaged cargo).

Grain, of course, came from the lower, arable land. The Island had great reaches of downland too. These were full of sheep, producing wool of a quality that was eagerly sought after, and the annual wool crop was taken up by clothiers as far afield as Kent and the Cotswolds, as well as serving a textile industry on the Island during the medieval period.

If all this sounds too good to be true, there was indeed a catch. Here was the only island close to the Channel coast that was both large enough to quarter an army and fertile enough to feed it. It is not surprising, then, that it occasionally attracted unwelcome visitors. The Island's archaeological record shows different ethnic and cultural migrations, and in the historical period the story is still of incomers, some benevolent and some hostile: the pagan Jutes, the Christian Saxons, the Danes, and indeed the Normans. William the Conqueror landed in Sussex but King Harold had expected a Norman invasion into the Solent and, through the summer of 1066, made his main camp on the Isle of Wight.

The Norman period

A period of stability might have been expected

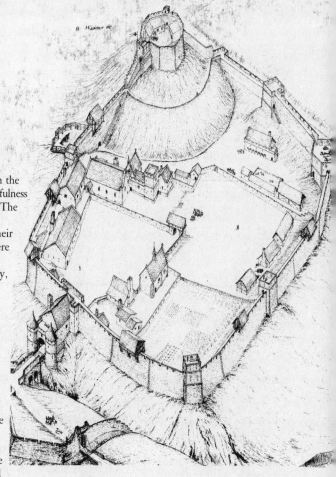

A bird's-eye view of Carisbrooke Castle near Newport, as it is supposed to have been in the reign of Edward III. Below: the Castle as it is today

after the Norman settlement, but the Island was not immune from the anarchy of Stephen's reign, and in 1136 Carisbrooke Castle underwent its first siege and its only capture in battle, because the springs failed due to a sudden drought.

The 13th century saw more invasion alarms. In 1267, expecting an attack by the younger Simon de Montfort, Henry III appointed the Countess Isabella to arrange an adequate guard of troops there. This royal announcement, however, conceals

more than it reveals. The Countess Isabella, mentioned in the letters patent, was one of the sharpest thorns in the royal side. Widowed in her mid-twenties, she had succeeded to great wealth and immense estates, including Carisbrooke Castle and much of the Isle of Wight, and she proceeded to rule the Island like a petty kingdom. With much expenditure of money she transformed Carisbrooke Castle from a military slum into something approaching an elegant residence.

Thus established in state, she maintained a life-style full of interest and action, including enjoying litigation against the Abbot of Quarr, the bailiff of Newport, or anyone else who crossed her path. Even the Crown trod carefully where Isabella was concerned – which made the planning of Island defence rather difficult. Troops could not be moved in unless they were Isabella's men, or unless they came with her permission.

The Crown bided its time. In 1293, when Isabella was dying, a royal agent arrived at her deathbed with an offer to buy her estates. The sale was made, and henceforth the Lords of the Island were not hereditary barons but Crown appointees with the defence of the area as their main charge.

The new arrangements came none too soon. During the 1290s relations with France became tense, and there was talk of threatened invasion as Islanders scurried around looking to their defences. This was no time for nice protocol about the movement of troops, and the English Crown must have been relieved to have some freedom of action in the Island. As at other times of military stress, internal communications on the Island gave some problems. In 1295, a particularly anxious year, nearly £89 was spent on road building.

French attacks

It was in the 14th century, however, that the Island was to see most of the military action as general hostilities with France developed. A successful French raid on some ships off the Island in 1336, was followed by the first serious attack on the Solent in 1338, with raids on Portsmouth in the spring, and Southampton in the autumn. The garrison at Carisbrooke Castle at this time was not very impressive: 6 men at arms, and 12 archers. By 1342 the number of archers had increased to 40.

The Treaty of Bretigny in 1360 brought a temporary peace, but when war was resumed in 1369 it was to bring a more intense threat to the Island. Landings were made in 1372 and 1374, but these were made to seem insignificant by the events of 1377 when a large French force attacked various points on the south coast of England.

The Island's turn came from mid-August to mid-September. Landing soldiers and horses on the north coast of the Island, the French army fanned out into the interior, leaving a trail of destruction as they went. They burned the church at Yarmouth, and destroyed Newtown and the much larger town of Newport (where the tax returns seem to show no population for the next two years). The action then moved to Carisbrooke Castle where the garrison was commanded by Hugh Tyrel. The castle defences proved equal to the test.

The story of the outcome of this siege was preserved in a local tradition, recorded in a 16th-century church register and a 17th-century diary. One of the castle garrison, an archer named Peter de Heynoe, observed that in the half-light each dawn and evening one of the besieging army would creep quite close to the west wall of the castle – the side containing the main gateway – evidently reconnoitring a possible way in. It was a risky venture, and the French scout paid the price; taking careful aim through his loophole, Peter de Heynoe shot and killed the Frenchman with a crossbow bolt. This was no mere scout, as it turned out, but the French commander, and the besieging force, discouraged, went away.

The following year saw them back again, this time with only a small raiding force which destroyed a mill and a priory near Newport.

So the war rumbled on. In December 1403 a French force of 1,000 men landed on the Island with the intention of spending Christmas there, and proceeded to round up cattle and sheep; but they were driven back to their ships by the local militia, who were no doubt incensed at the disappearance of their farm stock. In the summer of 1404 a larger force of 1,600 French landed and found an almost deserted landscape, as the Islanders

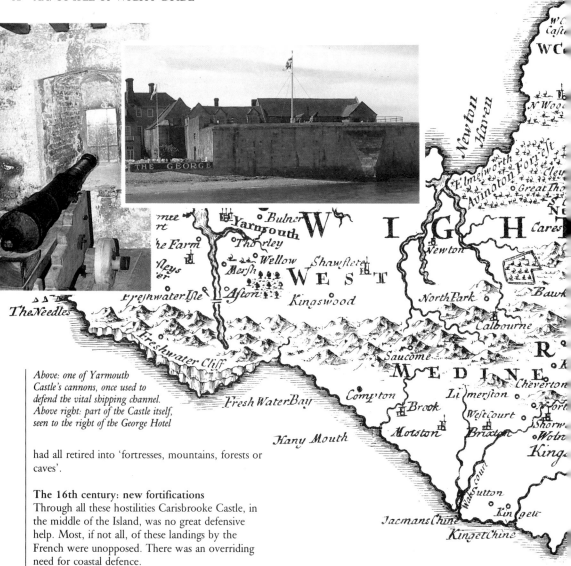

Above: one of Yarmouth Castle's cannons, once used to defend the vital shipping channel. Above right: part of the Castle itself, seen to the right of the George Hotel

had all retired into 'fortresses, mountains, forests or caves'.

The 16th century: new fortifications

Through all these hostilities Carisbrooke Castle, in the middle of the Island, was no great defensive help. Most, if not all, of these landings by the French were unopposed. There was an overriding need for coastal defence.

Several factors eventually flowed together to provide it. The improvement in artillery technique by the early 16th century strengthened the logic of having coastal forts, which promised to be effective. The efficient Tudor government machine offered the means; the suppression of the monastic houses in the 1530s provided the material, in terms both of finance and of masonry; and a foreign threat, again from France, offered the occasion.

The fortification scheme for the Island was only part of a chain of forts along the south and east coasts, but it was extensive enough. It would have been an even more formidable undertaking but for the help of geography. Landing conditions on much of the southern coast of the Island are often dangerous – as the long toll of shipwrecks over the centuries has testified – and only Sandown Bay seems an inviting way in on that side. It is the Solent shore of the Island that offers more in the way of creeks and inlets, and it was here that most of the forts were sited.

Building started in the late 1530s and was still in progress during the French raids on the Solent and the Island in 1545 when the *Mary Rose* foundered. There is every sign of the handiwork of a varied collection of engineers and surveyors. The fort at West Cowes, with its half-moon bastion, is in the German tradition; the forts at Sandown (then known as Sandham) and at Yarmouth reflected the new Italian fashion by having an arrowhead bastion to give flanking fire along the two landward faces of wall. There were simple octagonal sconces like Worsley's Tower, west of Yarmouth, and a square blockhouse with two corner flankers at Sharpnode, also near Yarmouth and helping to control the vital shipping channel between the Island and Hurst Castle.

There is evidence that some of these forts were built with more speed than care, and with scant attention to the foundations. West Cowes castle developed serious settlement cracks through its structure within 30 years, and the Island Captain reported with some exasperation that if any of the cannons were fired it would bring the fort down.

Local defence

By way of back-up to these fortifications there was the local defence system. By the 1500s the parishes had joined together for defence and for many administrative purposes into parish clusters called centons, each under a centoner who served as a local militia commander. There were 11 centons: five in East Medine (east of the River Medina), five in West Medine, and the town of Newport which constituted a centon of its own. In emergencies and for training, the West Medine militia would assemble on St George's Down, and the East Medine militia on Brading Down.

Internal communication was by means of hobblers, mounted soldiers who doubled as despatch riders, the key to any mobilisation of the militia was the signal beacon system, backed up by the ringing of church bells. The beacon system itself had flourished in the Island through the

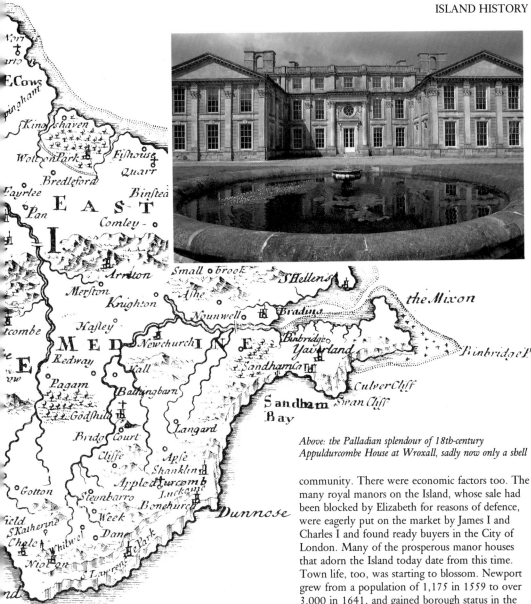

Above: the Palladian splendour of 18th-century Appuldurcombe House at Wroxall, sadly now only a shell

medieval period. In the 14th century there were 29 beacons – 13 in East Medine and 16 in West Medine – and, though the number varied, the system had been continuously maintained. By the 16th century the beacons were grouped in pairs, except at the key stations of the East and West Forelands, which were repeater stations for signals to and from the mainland, where there were three beacons in order to be able to indicate the degree of emergency. These Foreland stations were a vital part of the system because many of the mainland militia, and boats for their transport, were on standby to move help into the Island in the event of an enemy landing.

The weapons the militia could call upon included bows, spears, pikes, bills, calivers and arquebuses, and also the parish guns, field pieces on creaking carriages. In the 16th century the Island had 15 parish guns, comprising four falcons and 11 falconets, distributed among the various parishes.

Modern times

The Spanish Armada alarms in 1588 and subsequently through the 1590s were the last major cause for disturbance. Partly because of improved defence arrangements and partly because of a more settled political situation – even the English Civil War largely passed the Island by – there was a new confidence among the Island community. There were economic factors too. The many royal manors on the Island, whose sale had been blocked by Elizabeth for reasons of defence, were eagerly put on the market by James I and Charles I and found ready buyers in the City of London. Many of the prosperous manor houses that adorn the Island today date from this time. Town life, too, was starting to blossom. Newport grew from a population of 1,175 in 1559 to over 3,000 in 1641, and gained borough status in the process; and the new town of Cowes soon grew out of recognition from its modest beginnings in the 1540s.

Fuelling this growth was a mercantile-based industry. Baking and brewing had been quite modest staple trades in medieval times, but with the development of Newport harbour in the later 16th century, and the increasing traffic of shipping in the Solent generally, maritime provisioning became a lucrative business.

Growing wealth found some expression in architectural elegance. In the 18th century the Palladian splendour of Appuldurcombe House and even its more modest fellows, in such an Arcadian setting, began to draw tourist visitors of a genteel sort: including those who could afford the horse carriage and the services of a boy to open and close all the gates that so bedevilled progress along the rutted Island roads.

With the 19th century came the belated transport revolution: a Highways Act in 1813 offering better road surfaces, toll charges, and – more gates. Then, in the second half of the century, came railways galore. Of these, alas, only a small number remain, but they continue to serve the cause of tourism.

Dr Jack Jones was formerly Curator of Carisbrooke Castle Museum and is a historian with particular interest in the Isle of Wight.

The Making of Wight

T he Isle of Wight exhibits an unusual diversity of geology within a comparatively small area. Since the early 19th century the excellence of the geological exposures and the relative abundance of fossils in the local rocks have attracted a constant stream of professional and amateur investigators and collectors to the Island. In spite of this intensive study, new phenomena and fossils are still being discovered.

The topography of the Island is controlled by the underlying geology and by the recent geological history of the area. By the nature of the soils they produce, rocks influence vegetation and land use.

The Island is composed entirely of sedimentary rocks – that is, rocks laid down in approximately horizontal layers or beds under water. The local rocks preserve within them the evidence for the geological history of the area for about the last 120 million years. This history has three distinct phases: Cretaceous, Palaeogene and Quaternary.

The western tip of the Wight. Gravel capped Headon Warren overlooks the sands of Alum Bay and the chalk of The Needles

Dinosaurs and Chalk

120 million years ago, when the oldest rocks exposed on the Island were being laid down, the geography and climate of the area were very different from those of today. What is now the southern part of the Island and the adjacent English Channel was a broad valley through which a large river flowed towards the north-east. To the north of this valley lay a ridge of low hills. Periodic floods brought sands and muds down the river from the west to be deposited in the valley. These sands and muds now form the rock unit geologists call the Wealden Group. The Wealden Group rocks on the Island are one of the richest sources of dinosaur bones in Europe. These dinosaurs, mostly vegetarians, roamed through the luxuriant forests of conifers, tree ferns and cycads that grew in the drier areas.

About 110 million years ago the area began to change. A sea began to inundate the region from the south. The latest Wealden rocks were deposited in a vast lagoon and record the earliest phase of this change.

The Wealden Group rocks occur in two isolated areas, one north of Sandown and the other along the south-west coast. The deposits are mainly clays and on the coast rapid erosion takes place, producing relatively low, unstable cliffs. The Wealden clays produce heavy soils and most of the inland outcrop is given over to rough pasture.

The next part of the rock sequence, the Lower Greensand, Gault and Upper Greensand, was

THE MAKING OF WIGHT 15

deposited on the bottom of the shallow sea which had spread over southern England. The Lower Greensand consists mainly of sandstones with some clay seams. It underlies much of the southern half of the Island. Where this geological unit reaches the coast it forms high, terraced cliffs, as at Blackgang and Red Cliff. Inland it produces gently rolling country with isolated knolls and hog-back ridges. The Lower Greensand produces a light sandy soil which provides some of the best arable land on the Island.

The Gault and Upper Greensand together form a narrow strip immediately south of the central Chalk ridge and all around the southern downs. Although these two rock units have such a limited occurrence, they have a marked influence on the landscape. The Gault is a dark grey clay while the Upper Greensand is a hard, pale grey sandstone. This arrangement of a solid sandstone over a mechanically weak clay has resulted in some of the most extensive and spectacular landslips in Europe.

The final part of the Cretaceous story is recorded by a very thick sequence of grey and white limestones, the Chalk. This was deposited in a deepening sea and is composed largely of millions of microscopic algal remains. In the upper part of the Chalk occur layers of irregular flint nodules, which were used by the early inhabitants of the Island as raw material for making tools and weapons.

The Chalk forms the central 'backbone' of the Island. This is a narrow, steep-sided ridge except in the area west of Newport, where it broadens considerably. Where this ridge reaches the sea, at Culver in the east and in the west between Compton Bay and The Needles, the Chalk forms high, vertical cliffs. A second area of Chalk underlies the high downs between Shanklin and St Catherine's Point along the southern coast of the Island. The Chalk gives rise to a very thin lime-rich soil, which supports a distinctive vegetation. Although large areas of the Chalk outcrop are now under cultivation or afforested, there are still some areas where traditional methods of sheep-grazing maintain the typical downland habitat.

About 65 million years ago the sea retreated. All the Cretaceous rocks which had been laid down were gently buckled by earth movements. This series of events marks the end of the first phase of the geological history.

Sea and swamp
About 60 million years ago a new geography began to take shape. The sea began to inundate the eroded Chalk land surface. Across what is now the southern half of the Island was a ridge of low hills. The sea was restricted to the area north of these hills. For the next 30 million years or so, the shoreline of the sea constantly shifted as sea level fluctuated, as the land intermittently subsided and as a river built out a delta eastwards across the area. As a result the region was sometimes submerged under a warm, shallow sea, while at others it was a low-lying coastal swamp and marsh

Considering its relatively small area, the Isle of Wight contains a wide diversity of rock forms, as shown in this diagram. Vegetation and land use on the Island are greatly influenced by the underlying geology

Key
Palaeogene
Chalk
Gault and Upper Greensand
Lower Greensand
Wealden Group

crossed by numerous streams and dotted with lakes. These different environments laid down a succession of clays and sands which now lie beneath the northern half of the Island.

The Palaeogene beds have given rise to a region of generally low hills with gentle slopes down to the Solent, except in the west where steeper landslipped cliffs occur in places. The soils in the area are generally very heavy and difficult to cultivate without extensive underdrainage. For this reason, this is a region of grass meadow or woodland, although recently modern ploughing techniques have enabled some areas to be cultivated. The exception to this general picture is the region south-east of Yarmouth. Here, there is an extensive tract underlain by limestone and this produces light calcareous soils. Much of this area is under cultivation.

About 30 million years ago the sea retreated completely from the area. The whole rock sequence was then buckled by major earth movements which were associated with the formation of the Alps far to the south. Some of the originally horizontal strata now dip steeply as a result of this folding.

Variable climates

Very little evidence is preserved of the geological history of the Island for the last 30 million years. The whole area appears to have remained above sea level for almost all this period of time. The folded rocks were moulded and etched by the forces of weathering and erosion. In this way the landscape gradually evolved until about two million years ago, when conditions changed dramatically and the whole process speeded up.

About two million years ago, the climate began a series of relatively rapid changes. Although the detailed history of this, the Quaternary period, is not known for the Island, the general features are well established. Periodically, average annual temperatures fell to such a level that glaciers and ice sheets developed in the northern hemisphere. There were, perhaps, as many as 20 of these Ice-Ages or glacials, each lasting about 100,000 years. The glacials were separated by warmer periods termed interglacials. During these interglacials, average annual temperatures were as high as or even higher than they are today.

During the glacials, while the ice sheets did not reach as far south as the Isle of Wight, the climate locally would have resembled that of Arctic Canada. At the same time, sea level fell so that the English Channel was dry land. The lowered sea level had an important effect; it caused the local rivers to deepen their valleys. During the interglacials, as the ice sheets melted, sea level rose, flooding the over-deepened river valleys.

About 10,000 years ago the present interglacial phase began. The climate improved and sea level rose. About 8,000 years ago the sea had flooded all the local river valleys and had broken through the Chalk ridge which had formerly continued from the Island westwards to Dorset. The Island had finally become an island. Since that time, continuing sea level change, coastal erosion and river valley deposition have between them produced the Island as we see it today.

The chines

A distinctive feature of the southern coast of the Island is the number of stream valleys locally known as chines. The word 'chine' is derived from an Anglo-Saxon word *cine*, which meant a fissure or ravine. The Island chines are produced by a combination of rapid coastal erosion and continuous stream down-cutting. Although the mechanism of formation is the same in each case, the chines are not uniform in character but vary according to the nature of the rocks in which they are excavated and also the local climate.

Those chines eroded in the Lower Greensand tend to be relatively narrow and steep-sided. In the case of Shanklin Chine, erosion has produced a winding, very steep ravine, while Whale Chine is almost straight. Blackgang Chine is still a spectacular spot but it was once the largest of all the Island chines. Over the decades, rapid erosion has removed all of the seaward end of this chine.

The Needles

The chalk sea-stacks known as The Needles are probably one of the most instantaneously recognisable features of the British coastline. They owe their origin to a local peculiarity of the geology. Within the upper part of the Chalk here there is an unusually hard band of rock. Over the centuries the sea has worn away the surrounding softer limestone, leaving behind the remnants of the hard band like a row of broken teeth. Today there are just three conspicuous stacks, but there was once a fourth one, which may have been responsible for the name of the group. This fourth sea-stack was a slender pinnacle about 120ft (40m) high and was known as 'Lot's Wife'. In 1764 it fell, the noise, it is said, being heard for miles around. The innermost stack was originally joined to the mainland by an arch but this collapsed in about 1815.

The Alum Bay coloured sands

The spectacular coloured sands occur in the central part of Alum Bay, where they are interspersed with clays in vertical layers. There are five main colours (white, black, green, red and yellow-brown) but with many different shades. The variety of colour is produced by minor amounts of accessory minerals in the sands. The sands are made up of grains of the mineral quartz (chemically silicon dioxide). Quartz is a colourless mineral and pure quartz sands are therefore white. The addition of various mineral impurities to a white quartz sand can produce great variation in colour.

The black and grey sands are produced by the inclusion of minute particles of carbon in the sands. The carbon was originally partly decomposed plant debris which was incorporated within the sand as it was being laid down millions of years ago.

Most of the colours are due to the green mineral called glauconite, which is either still in the sand today or was originally present. Glauconite is a complex potassium, iron and aluminium silicate, which was formed when the sands were deposited some 45 million years ago. If glauconite is present in the sand, it produces a grey-green to deep green colour, depending on the amount included. However, glauconite is unstable when exposed to weathering and decomposes to form several different iron minerals. These iron minerals include the yellow to brown oxide limonite and the red oxide haematite. By altering the proportions of these minerals in the sand, a whole range of yellow, brown and red hues can be produced.

The Undercliff

Much of the coastal area of the Island is subject to

Dramatic Ladder Chine is one of several land faults to be seen along the Island's south coast cliffs

Numerous logs of fossilised wood (some beautifully preserved) form the unusual 'Pine Raft' at Hanover Point

Landslip blocks

Chalk

Upper Greensand

Gault Clay acts as a lubricant to the overlying layers and causes cliff falls

Gault

Sea Level

Curved rupture surfaces

Lower Greensand

landslips, but the most spectacular lie between Shanklin and Chale, the area known as the Undercliff. The repeated landslips here have been produced because of the local geological sequence: porous Chalk and Upper Greensand overlying impermeable Gault Clay. The latter is known locally, with good reason, as the 'Blue Slipper'.

Landslips occur because there are curved rupture surfaces within the Gault Clay. When the rupture surface becomes lubricated by water percolating down from the surface, movement is liable to occur. Masses of Chalk, Upper Greensand and Gault move seawards on the rupture or slip surface. Since the movement takes place on a curved slip surface, as the block slides seawards, so the layering in the rocks is rotated so that it comes to tilt steeply inland.

Although large-scale movements still take place in the Undercliff – the last one was at Blackgang in 1978 – the really big slips occurred probably hundreds of years ago. Repeated landslips have resulted in the distinctive terraced landscape of the area, each terrace representing a single slip. The inland boundary of the Undercliff is marked by a vertical cliff, more noticeable towards the west. Everything seaward of this cliff has been involved in land movement to a greater or lesser extent. In fact the Undercliff is the largest area of coastal landslip in north-western Europe.

The topography and location of the Undercliff, sandwiched as it is between the sea and the steeply rising downs, conspire to produce a very localised climate. The whole coastal strip is very sheltered and hence tends to be warmer in winter than other parts of the Island. The Undercliff is also prone to

sea mists, moisture condensing out of the onshore breezes as they rise up over the downs. Plants grow well here and the tumbled landscape is thickly clothed in gnarled oaks covered in ivy and clematis, while underfoot are rich carpets of ferns and mosses. It was the resulting picturesque quality of this landscape that initially attracted the early visitors to the area. Later, Ventnor was to develop out of a tiny fishing hamlet because the peculiarities of the climate made it an ideal winter resort.

Hanover Point 'Pine Raft'

Hanover Point is the headland between Brook and Compton Bays. It is the site of the so-called 'Pine Raft', an unusual geological phenomenon.

At low tide, a sandstone reef is exposed on the foreshore seaward of the point. Scattered around the western side of this reef are numerous logs of fossilised wood, some up to 12ft (4m) long. Unfortunately the logs are not easy to see because they are usually obscured by a thick growth of seaweed. The logs do not represent a fossil forest since there is no evidence that they grew where they were buried. Instead they accumulated as a log jam when the river was in flood. Most of the wood is identifiable as that of a primitive conifer. Some of it is beautifully preserved and exhibits annular growth rings.

In the beds around Hanover Point many dinosaur footprints and trackways have been discovered in recent years.

Dr Allan Insole is a geologist specialising in the geology of the Island. He is also Museum Officer for the Isle of Wight County Council.

Nature's Garden Isle

The Isle of Wight has been given many alternative names for various reasons, but none has been more long-lasting and appropriate than the 'Garden Isle' in recognition of its natural beauty.

One would expect the Island to be different from the mainland and so it is, but in a subtle and important way, although this may not immediately be apparent. Certainly there are rarities not found elsewhere in Britain, such as the wood calamint and Glanville fritillary butterfly, but these are not likely to be seen by most people. What is much more important is the variety of scenery, so many different kinds of habitat, each with its own distinctive plants and animals, that are represented there. If you come from anywhere in south-east England, you will surely find some part of the Island which is just like home. This is the secret. Owing to its varied geology the Island is a microcosm of all that is found in south-east England (and a bit more beside), compressed and squeezed into an area less than one-tenth the size of Hampshire.

In order to obtain the maximum benefit from this compactness and variety, you should make full use of the network of well-marked footpaths and bridleways, amounting to some 500 miles, giving access to almost every corner of the Island. To pass from one sort of habitat to another you need walk only a short distance on the Island, when it might involve a journey of several miles on the mainland.

In simple terms, the Isle of Wight is dominated

Main picture: just one of the beautiful sun-dappled walks that can be enjoyed in Parkhurst Forest, once a royal hunting forest. Inset: in spring, wild daffodils can be seen in many of the Island's woods

by the chalk ridge forming the 'backbone' of downs from The Needles in the west to Culver Cliff in the east. To the north of this ridge the soil is mostly heavy Tertiary clays, overlaid in places with Pleistocene gravels, while to the south the underlying sands and clays produce light, well-drained soils with a characteristic warm brown colour. In the southernmost part of the Island there is a second group of downs from Shanklin to St Catherine's, including the highest point of the Island on St Boniface Down at 787ft (240m).

The various habitats we can see today are the result of the combined effects of geology, the physical and chemical properties of soil, aspect and weather, and the subtle inter-relationships of living plants and animals, including most importantly the human influence and use of land. The purpose of these notes is to indicate where these habitats may be found and some of the interesting plants and animals associated with them.

Woodland

When the Island was separated from the mainland some 7,000 years ago, like most of lowland Britain it would have been almost completely covered with deciduous forest. From Neolithic times much of this was cleared by early settlers from the chalk downs and parts of the south, but even in medieval times most of the north was still well wooded. Parkhurst Forest and Borthwood, much larger than they are today, were designated as royal hunting forests with red and fallow deer, now long extinct. Demands for timber by the ship-building industry at Portsmouth depleted the Island forests, which were sadly neglected until the Forestry Commission took over their management in 1919 with beneficial results. As they did elsewhere, they planted softwoods, but only in comparatively small stands, and they still maintained areas of deciduous woodland and coppice, thus increasing the diversity and interest. They also created a new forest at Brighstone, where beech was interplanted with pine from the late 1930s. Most of the pine has recently been taken out, so that by the year 2000 there should be 1,000 acres of mature beech forest. Parkhurst Forest, Firestone Copse and Brighstone Forest all have ample car parks, but space for cars

is limited at Borthwood and Combley Great Wood. All are well worth visiting.

Recognisable remnants of ancient forest are hard to find, but the wood cricket, a very local insect closely associated with woodland, is found in parts of Borthwood, Parkhurst and Firestone, but not in Brighstone. It is also found in the New Forest and seems to indicate at least a long history of continuous woodland habitat where it is found. It is not easy to see in the leaf litter, but the churring of several males can readily be heard.

There is always something of interest to see in a wood. In many deciduous woods and copses there are striking displays of spring flowers – wild daffodils, wood anemones and bluebells – in rapid succession before the leaves come on the trees and block out the light. Wide rides and fire-breaks let in the light and increase the woodland edge to the benefit of other woodland flowers, butterflies and birds. The lovely narrow-leaved lungwort, a very local plant, grows in many woods. Mosses, ferns and lichens abound, especially in the older woods. The lack of ground cover in pine-woods is made up for by the large conical nests of the fiercesome wood ant (not a good place to choose to picnic), which are often raided by woodpeckers. In the autumn the woods are bright with mushrooms and toadstools in great variety.

The native red squirrel is still present in most woods. Both fox and badger, although introduced, are now common and widespread, but the badger favours the sandy areas in the south. Stoats and weasels may well be seen. There are good populations of dormice and wood mice, but you are less likely to see these than the signs of their presence, since they only come out at night. Bank voles and common and pygmy shrews are active by day and may well be seen, or more likely heard in the case of the latter. Ten of the 15 species of native bats have been recorded since 1980, including three separate records of the very rare Bechstein's bat, a woodland species, in 1986.

Downland

The Tennyson Monument on High Down, Freshwater, was erected in memory of the famous poet who lived at Farringford in the valley below and frequently walked the downs, declaring that the air was 'worth sixpence a pint'. The monument also serves as a beacon to sailors along this dangerous coast and is an irresistible lure to walkers determined to reach the top. Thousands do and are rewarded with unrivalled views in all directions. If

Main picture: a view over the green and rolling Ashey Down from where the sea mark can be seen in the far distance. Inset: the beautiful wild pyramidal orchid is one of the gems of the downland

you look down from the edge of the cliff, you can see how the poet was inspired to write that magic line – 'The wrinkled sea beneath him crawls.' It is exactly right.

One might have thought that the tramp of so many feet would lead to serious erosion, but such is not the case. In fact the precious downland turf, probably the best in England, is actually improved and maintained by this traffic. Soft yet firm, smooth and dry even after rain, this is indeed the lawn in Nature's Garden. A closer examination shows that it is not composed only of grass, but contains lots of tiny plants with dainty coloured flowers of many kinds – wild thyme, marjoram, centaury, clustered bellflower, salad burnet, eyebright and squinancy-wort. This is a manmade habitat to which these plants, which may grow quite tall in the valley, have adapted by growing small and pressing close to the ground to conserve moisture and avoid exposure to the wind. Further away from the sea and wind the plants grow taller, and include such gems as orchids of many kinds (which should, of course, never be picked). Further away still, viper's-bugloss and nettle-leaved bellflower compete for attention and chalk scrub turns inevitably to woodland if left unchecked.

Much of the chalk downland belongs to the National Trust, and nearly all of it is readily accessible. You will find examples of every type of chalkland habitat, from sublime to completely disastrous, resulting from past and present usage – a veritable textbook of chalkland ecology.

The downland plants are very attractive to many butterflies such as common, chalkhill, small and Adonis blues, skippers, graylings, dark green fritillaries and many more. The warm, dry conditions are particularly suitable for grasshoppers of many kinds, whose cheerful chirruping heralds a sunny day. Rabbits, sometimes of an unusual ginger colour or wholly black, and hares will frequently be seen. Kestrels hover over the downs watching for field voles.

Farmland

It is much to the credit of Island farmers that the countryside is as interesting and attractive as it is today. Although changes in farming practices have left their mark, the Island seems to have escaped the worst excesses of intensive food production. Some hedges have been lost, but many have been retained and even new ones planted, much to the benefit of hedgerow birds and other forms of wildlife. Since the great drought of 1976, many farmers have excavated large reservoirs, adding considerably to the stock of farm ponds. These can only be of benefit to wildlife in general and some of them have already been adopted by frogs, toads and the three species of newt which are widespread in the Island.

Many farmers are now in the forefront of the conservation movement, opening their farms to allow school parties and members of the public to see what is being done to encourage wildlife, while still running a commercially viable farm. They are well worth a visit and deserve our support and encouragement.

Cliffs and chines

The plants growing on the white chalk cliffs between Freshwater Bay and Compton give a special meaning to our chosen title. This is a good place to find the hoary stock with magenta flowers and a delicious scent from May to July, which is almost certainly the native wild plant from which the Brompton stocks in our gardens were developed. Close by there are several plants of wild cabbage, from which most of the 'greens' in our vegetable gardens were bred. On the chalk cliffs to the west of Freshwater Bay there are cascades of familiar wallflowers, but these are not wild. They have escaped from cultivation and find the conditions here much more to their liking. Another striking plant which has almost certainly escaped from gardens and gone wild is the red valerian, also found here on old walls.

From Compton eastwards to St Catherine's Point the softer cliffs of sand and clay slump down to the sea to form an ever-changing series of undercliffs with temporary ponds much used by amphibians. This is one of the main breeding areas of the Glanville fritillary and also the first landfall for migratory butterflies such as painted ladies and clouded yellows, which in good years, like 1983, appear in enormous numbers. It is also a good area for bush-crickets of many kinds, including the great green bush-cricket whose strident call is a common sound south of the chalk.

At intervals along this coast small streams cut narrow ravines in the soft strata, which the wind has later scooped out to form what are known locally as 'chines'. Some are still only small, but Whale Chine is most impressive and well worth a visit . Blackgang Chine has suffered greatly from erosion recently and owes its popularity to commercial enterprise. Beyond Blackgang the cliffs are highly unstable: major landslides occurred in 1928 and 1978. The tumbled land here and around St Catherine's Lighthouse is rich in wildlife and an important observation point for migratory birds.

From Niton to Luccombe, massive landslides in the more distant past have resulted in a more stable Undercliff, known as such as far as Ventnor and beyond Bonchurch as the 'Landslip'. Although much of it has been built on, the area is still of outstanding interest. Fully exposed to the sun and protected from cold northerly winds by the inner cliff, it has a Mediterranean climate, as can be seen by the range of tender plants growing in the open at the Ventnor Botanical Gardens on the site of the former Royal National Hospital at St Lawrence. The whole area is a tumbled mass of giant chalk

and rock boulders interspersed with mixed soils so that chalk-loving and lime-hating plants jostle with each other for position, creating what can only be described as Nature's Rock Garden. The European wall lizard *Podarcis muralis* occurs on walls and in gardens in the centre of Ventnor. At Shanklin another impressive chine is especially good for ferns, mosses and liverworts.

In the north of the Island, except where rocky promontories occur, the rate of erosion is considerable, as can be seen by the litter of trees and shrubs on the muddy shore. Headon Warren in the west is our best example of dwarf shrub heath, a favourite spot for native reptiles, but the smooth snake and sand lizard are absent. Further to the west the unique coloured sands of Alum Bay lead to the chalk cliffs of The Needles headland, the home of many interesting seabirds.

Rivers and wetlands

Apart from a few short streams in the south, the principal rivers flow northwards into the Solent. The Medina and the Eastern Yar rise in the southern downs, the former flowing through Newport to Cowes, and the latter winding its way to Bembridge Harbour. The Western Yar rises close to the sea at Freshwater Bay and joins the Solent at Yarmouth. A number of smaller streams combine to form the tidal creeks at Wootton and Newtown. Although much robbed for water supplies, there are good stretches of river at Alverstone, Gatcombe, Carisbrooke and Calbourne Mill. Strangely, the minnow is absent from the Island. Water voles are widespread, but the status of the otter is now doubtful.

Wetlands of different kinds are associated with these rivers. Good for dragonflies are freshwater marshes such as Alverstone, Brading and Bembridge in the east, largely on private land, and Afton Marsh, Freshwater, a small area of typical

sheltered, but there are interesting shingle spits at Hamstead and King's Quay, while sand spits occur at Norton, Yarmouth, and St Helen's Duver, which incidentally has a richer flora than anywhere else of a similar area. In the south the shores are more often composed of sand or shingle. Rocky shores – such as at Freshwater Bay, Hanover Point, near Brook, Horse Ledge, Shanklin, Bembridge Foreland, St Helens and Seaview – are the most productive of marine life. Owing to its central position at the entrance to Southampton Water, the Island is fortunate in having not only the Channel species typical of the south coast, but also some Atlantic species, such as the flat top shell, two species of limpet and the snakelocks anemone, which reach the easterly limit of their range here. These are further augmented by foreign species brought in accidentally by shipping from as far away as Australia and Japan. Most do no harm and are welcome additions to the native marine life, but some can cause problems. One of these is the now widespread Japanese Seaweed *Sargassum muticum*, first recorded at Bembridge in 1973.

As in the other habitats described, there is much of great interest to be found on the shore – but please check on the tides before you go exploring – it is easy to get cut off.

Oliver H Frazer is leader of the Mammals, Reptiles and Amphibians section of the Isle of Wight Natural History and Archaeological Society. He photographs and lectures on the natural history of the Island.

Top picture: tree lupins at St Helen's Duver, which is particularly rich in different types of plants. Above: boary stock flowers on the chalk cliffs from May to July.
Above right: adder with young. These heath-dwelling reptiles use their poison to immobilise more active prey.
Right: great green bush-cricket

fen, which is a Local Nature Reserve with a Nature Trail. Owing to the domination of the chalk, there are only a few small areas of acid bog, with characteristic plants, in the region of Godshill.

Tidal estuaries, good for birdlife, occur between Newport and Cowes, at Yarmouth, and particularly at Newtown, where the saltmarsh is coloured by thrift, sea-lavender, sea aster and golden samphire in their seasons. This, too, is a Local Nature Reserve, mostly owned by the National Trust.

Coast and seashore
The varied coastline of about 60 miles in length gives rise to many different types of shore according to the substrata, aspect and exposure to prevailing winds. Generally speaking, the shores on the north coast tend to be muddy and well

Flotsam, Jetsam and Lagan

If there is one edifice on the Isle of Wight that stands as a monument to smuggling, shipwrecks and lighthouses, it is the 14th-century pharos (the lighthouse known locally as the 'Pepper Pot') on St Catherine's Hill, 774ft (236m) above sea level. Equally it is a monument to the folly of one man, Walter de Goditon, who believed that he could safely abscond with 53 casks of white wine, out of a total cargo of 174, from the wreck of the *Ship of the Blessed Mary* from Aquitaine, which struck at Atherfield Ledge on the south-west coast of the Island in 1313.

The wine belonged to a religious community in Normandy, and Walter was therefore committing an offence not only against the Church of Rome, but also against Edward II, who was then attempting to maintain peace with his Continental neighbours. After a long and complicated trial, Walter was fined 267½ marks and 20 marks damages. The legend is that he was also ordered by the Church, as an act of expiation and a token of contrition, to build a pharos and oratory on the site of an earlier hermitage and chantry, and to maintain a warning light in the pharos for mariners at sea, and to appoint 'a chaunting priest to sing

masses for the soul of Walter, his ancestors and those at sea'. They were built in 1323.

Externally the pharos is octagonal, surmounted by a pyramidal roof, the whole structure being 35½ft (10.5m) high, but inside there are only four walls, each of which is four feet thick. There are two entrances, one above the other, and around the top of the tower are openings to allow a light to show. Although the oratory was destroyed in the dissolution of the chantries, the lighthouse itself was operational until 1638.

A short distance away on St Catherine's Hill is another partially built lighthouse known as the 'Mustard Pot'. This lighthouse was begun in 1785, but discontinued because of the high cost incurred and because of the belated realisation that its warning light would rarely be visible to sailors through fog and cloud, and was therefore of no practical use. Why this problem was not foreseen is a mystery.

Nothing more was done for many years to replace these obsolete structures although the south coast was notorious in the days of sailing ships for shipwrecks and deaths by drowning. It took a great marine tragedy, the wreck of the *Clarendon* in 1836, to awaken the consciences of Islanders to the desperate need for a new lighthouse on St Catherine's Point. Before that period they had tended to regard ships' cargoes deposited upon their shores as legitimate marine harvests and the loss of life at sea as merely regrettable.

Flotsam, jetsam and lagan

In the 13th and 14th centuries, the law distinguished different categories of goods that ended up in the sea. Goods from shipwrecks which

Huge seas drove the fully-rigged West Indiaman the Clarendon *ashore near Blackgang Chine in 1836, smashing her to pieces; only three crewmen were saved.*
Inset: St Catherine's Oratory, near cows

floated to land were *legal wreck*. Goods cast overboard at sea were either *jetsam* (if they sank) or *flotsam* (if they remained afloat). *Lagan* (or *ligan*) was yet another category of goods, those deliberately sunk in the sea, tied to corks or buoys so that they could later be recovered.

From 1266 onwards, merchant seamen were supposed to observe international law based upon the evidence of merchants on the custom of the sea, and disputes of 'migratory litigants' were tried in local courts. It was suggested that ships carried the law with them as part of their cargo, and an admiral from one of the Cinque Ports operated as a kind of itinerant Justice. It was laid down that the king protected strangers from assault and robbery, as well as all vessels wrecked on shore if man or dog or cat survived.

Despite the law, deliberate wrecking of ships along the southern shores of the Island took place as recently as the 18th century. Ships sailing along the Channel were deliberately lured on to the rocks by moving lights that looked like those of other vessels. Survivors from the wrecks were clubbed to death to eliminate evidence and silence witnesses.

The wreck of the *Clarendon*

The wreck that shocked Islanders into new concern for the safety of mariners took place on 11 October 1836. The *Clarendon* was fully rigged when a violent storm drove her on to the cliffs of Chale Bay. Watchers from the shore could only look on in horror as the vessel drove on to the rocks, her rigging crashing down on those on deck, the splintering and groaning of her timbers

drowning the shrieks of the terrified passengers.

In spite of the violence of the sea, one of the watchers, a fisherman and ex-naval man called John Wheeler, tied a rope round his waist and waded out among the wreckage to save three men. By a strange coincidence, one survivor, named Thompson, was a former shipmate of Wheeler's in the Navy; another was an Irishman, and a third a Scotsman. These were the only people saved from the wreck; 21 drowned. One girl was washed ashore at Southsea below her father's house.

A witness of the wreck, writing 50 years later in 1886, recalled hearing above the din of the storm a cacophony of musical discords as the piano aboard plunged about the deck when the vessel was thrown against the cliffs. Later, sheet music and other papers, reduced to pulp, were washed ashore. Among the other items salvaged, he recalled, were women's dresses, a Bill of Exchange for a large sum of money (which a Bristol firm honoured after it dried out), and an eight-day clock which had suffered no more damage than a broken glass-face. When cleaned, the clock worked perfectly for many years at Chale, and was later taken to the USA where it continued to do good service.

Islanders were so shocked by this disaster that work was begun almost immediately on the lighthouse at St Catherine's Point.

Smuggling and smugglers

In the 14th century, fine quality English wool was in great demand on the Continent, and much of it was smuggled from these shores. One such incident

Heave! Eighteenth-century 'salvage experts' hauling contraband liquor ashore in the shadow of Blackgang Chine

is noted in *Wykeham's Register* on 4 February 1395, when a member of the clergy was involved. A writ of summons was issued against the Rector of Freshwater, Thomas Symonde, on the charge of smuggling wool into France, and on 12 March there was 'a citation of the Rector to appear to said writ under pain of sequestration'. Wool smuggling was known as 'owling', doubtless because it was carried out at night under cover of darkness. 'Owling' continued unabated until the 18th century, when kegs of liquor, previously used as ballast by smugglers on their runs from France, superseded wool in importance commercially.

By the 18th century, smuggling was so alarmingly on the increase that in 1733 new laws governing the selection of juries were enacted by Parliament. One of the first smugglers to be convicted after the new laws were passed was Daniel Boyce, a local blacksmith.

Boyce was born at Alverstoke, Stokes Bay, and he displayed amazing talents as a smuggler, operating in partnership with another local man named Hatch, who lived at Berry near Stokes Bay. Between them they accumulated a fortune, and in the 1720s Boyce built Appley House, a luxurious mansion near Ryde. Beneath it he built vast cellars to store contraband liquor. Hatch was similarly placed on the other side of the Solent.

Although many people were aware of the source of Boyce's wealth, the courts were unable to convict him because he invariably bribed witnesses involved in the trials, and also the jurors, who until 1733 were selected by the sheriff of the county. If the sheriff himself was open to bribery, he could rig the jury and turn the trial into a farce, as happened in the case of Boyce.

The new laws introduced in 1733 addressed this problem by having the names of jurors chosen at random out of a container, a system less easy to abuse. Boyce and Hatch were eventually found guilty and sentenced to a term of imprisonment in the Fleet prison. Boyce died in 1740 and his home, Appley House, then passed into the hands of

Henry Roberts, whose widow in 1754 entertained Henry Fielding, the novelist and author of *A Voyage to Lisbon*, during a short visit to the Island.

Fielding describes how Boyce made £40,000 from his smuggling, and with part of this amount purchased the estate: 'and, by chance, probably, fixed on this spot for building a large house. Perhaps the convenience of carrying on his business, to which it is so well adapted, might dictate the situation to him. We can hardly attribute it to the same taste with which he furnished the house, or at least his library, by sending an order to a bookseller in London to pack him up five hundred pounds' worth of his handsomest books. . . .'

When he was sent to the Fleet, all Boyce's effects were sold by auction at Portsmouth for a very small price. The books he had purchased in bulk from London were almost worthless, 'for the bookseller was now discovered to have been perfectly a master of his trade, and, relying on Mr Boyce's finding little time to read, had sent him not only the most lasting wares of his shop, but duplicates of the same, under different titles'. So much for Boyce, the blacksmith, smuggler and self-styled bibliophile.

In West Wight there was one outstanding family in the history of Island smuggling, the Conway brothers, who once lived at Middleton Cottage, Middleton, Freshwater. A relative of theirs, the late Gertrude Turner, once told me of their nocturnal activities; how often she would hear taps on the windows in the middle of the night. The brothers used to carry two tubs at a time up an old cliff-face track below where the existing Tennyson monument stands. She was told that on one occasion a tub fell and smashed on the rocks 500ft (152m) below, and the smell of neat brandy carried for a great distance. They were afraid the coastguards would detect it, but they were lucky. Miss Turner said it was one of her duties after a run, to burn the ropes that tied the tubs together, and she showed me the crude compass that the brothers used on their trips to and from France.

Changing attitudes
Much money could be earned salvaging cargoes and timber from ships wrecked here, and it was not unusual for local children to seek credit from the Brighstone shopkeeper by promising: 'Mother will pay next shipwreck.'

The two men who were largely responsible for the change of heart that transformed local inhabitants from wreckers and smugglers to the nucleus of the first lifeboat crews were the Reverend McCall and Charles Seeley. The former aroused residents' consciences to Christian compassion for shipwrecked mariners, and the latter provided the wherewithal in property and lifeboats. The crucial year was 1860, when the first lifeboats were launched from Brook and Brighstone. The first coxswain of the Brighstone boat was a former smuggler, James Buckett, who had just completed nearly five years compulsory service in the Navy as a punishment for his crimes. Now a reformed man, Buckett proved to be a fine leader and a seaman of great skill and courage. A third lifeboat was launched later at Atherfield and was crewed almost entirely by the Cotton family.

Richard Hutchings has written several books on different aspects of the Isle of Wight and is also president of the Farringford Tennyson Society.

Island Celebrities

*I*s there no one who is commonplace here? Is
everybody either a poet, or a genius, or a painter,
or peculiar in some way?
(Hester Thackeray Fuller, *Three Freshwater Friends*,
Isle of Wight County Press, 1933)

The Isle of Wight has not always been kind to
strangers. Even now there is a certain reserve at
first between inhabitants and visitors – 'caulkheads'
and 'grockles' – while all those who live but were
not born there are forever categorised as 'overners'.

It was not until the 19th century that the Island
became a holiday resort, an English Riviera which
attracted great painters and writers in search of
unspoilt scenery and a sense of liberation. Before, it
had been an often hostile place, at times a prison.
While incarcerated at Carisbrooke Castle, Charles I
wrote a poem foretelling his imminent demise.

Another poet detained against his will was
William Davenant, Shakespeare's godson – some
allege his real son – who was imprisoned at Cowes
Castle (now, more agreeably, the Royal Yacht
Squadron) and there wrote his famous drama
Gondibert.

Local celebrities

There could scarcely be a greater contrast with
poets than 'Robert Holmes, Warrior', as his effigy
proclaims, who fought (in a polite excuse for
piracy) in the Dutch Wars, and returned in
triumph to the Island to become Governor.

Meanwhile, the scientist Robert Hooke, a man
of 'a crooked body with a sharp ingenious look'
was inventing diving bells and watch springs, as
well as naming the cell as the basis of living matter.
Hooke was born and raised in Freshwater; a
farmhouse on what was soon to be named Hooke
Hill was later rebuilt as the beautiful thatched
church of St Agnes at Freshwater Bay.

Knighton Gorges, near Arreton, was the setting
for a Hellfire Club which included Sir Joshua
Reynolds, the portrait painter, the actor David
Garrick, and John Wilkes, arch-agitator and owner
of a bizarre residence in Sandown now swept away
by the sea. Knighton Gorges met a similar
downfall. So that it would not pass to his daughter,
whose marriage displeased him, the owner, Maurice
Bisset, had the fine old building demolished.

With another of those ironies with which history
abounds, Knighton Gorges was the setting of Leigh
Richmond's *The Dairyman's Daughter*, an
improving religious tract about the death of a girl
who ends her moral young days interred in
Brading churchyard. The nearby waxworks
museum records (as well as Queen Victoria tapping
her foot and George Bernard Shaw riding a new-
fangled penny farthing) the immoral life of Sophie
Dawes. Born in St Helens, she became the lover
and murderer of the Duc de Bourbon before
returning to the Island in pious old age.

Wight abounds in such scandals. Near Newport
is Mical Morey's Hump, where the gentleman so
commemorated was hanged for the murder of his

*Still not amused: regally attired Queen Victoria is to be
seen sternly tapping her foot in Brading Wax Museum*

grandson. Part of the gallows survives as a roof
beam in the nearby Horse and Hounds.

Famous visitors

As communications with the mainland improved,
the Island became a more pleasing port of call, a
place of romance and artistic inspiration. It was
here that the young J M W Turner painted his first
oil, a study of fishing boats off The Needles, as
well as a succession of pencil sketches of coastal
scenes. Turner returned, older and famous, in 1827
to stay at East Cowes Castle – now demolished –
the ruggedly picturesque residence of the architect
John Nash, whose best memorial on the Island is
Newport Town Hall, now the Law Courts.
William Wordsworth, after a visit in 1793, 'left
the place with melancholy forebodings' of a war
with the French. He had been conducted round
Carisbrooke Castle by an aged guide who bore up
the dying General Wolfe at Quebec.

Carisbrooke also exerted its spell on John Keats.
He is said to have recited the opening lines of the
newly written *Endymion* in its grounds to his
friend, J H Reynolds, now buried nearby in
Church Litten. Turner himself painted a
commanding watercolour of the Castle Gatehouse
– Bembridge windmill also caught his eye. His
disciple Ruskin's philosophy endures at Bembridge
School, founded according to his principles of
Sacrifice, Truth, Beauty, Life, Memory and
Obedience. The school is guardian to the finest

An 1874 'Vanity Fair' drawing of the shameless poet Swinburne, who lived for a time at Bonchurch

Ruskin museum in the world. Another famous educator, Thomas Arnold of Rugby, was born in Cowes, where his father was Collector of Customs. Horatio Nelson stopped off in St Helens on his way to routing the French fleet at the Battle of the Nile.

It is to artists and writers, however, that Wight bequeathed its finest bargains, those of peace and solitude. George Morland fled from London to escape creditors, and painted some of his finest pictures, replete with smugglers and smoky taprooms, in the West Wight. He soon attracted the attention of the locals; he was arrested as a spy, and his sketch of a spaniel was claimed to be a map of the Island, cunningly disguised.

A less hostile reception was accorded to the mystical painter John Martin – who discerned doom in Freshwater Bay – and, later, the more cheerful work of Berthe Morisot, the sole female among the early French Impressionists.

The 19th century proved to be a Golden Age for English literature, and its greatest exponents all lived on or visited the Isle of Wight and, more specifically, three small and isolated villages: Shanklin, Bonchurch and Freshwater.

It was to Eglantine Cottage, Shanklin, that John Keats repaired on his second visit to the Island, in the summer of 1819. On his first visit he had briefly encountered South Wight and it was during a walk through Luccombe Chine that he composed his famous sonnet 'On the Sea':

It keeps eternal whisperings around
Desolate shores, and with its mighty swell
Gluts twice ten thousand caverns . . .

Now he came at greater leisure to feast his eyes 'upon the wideness of the Sea', as well as improve his health. And yet he knew he was engaged in a race against time. During these two months he wrote *The Pot of Basil* and *St Agnes Eve* as well as part of *Lamia* and *Hyperion*, but complained in a letter to Fanny Brawne of his 'little coffin of a room' and even confessed 'I am getting a great dislike of the picturesque'. Within two years he was dead, at the age of 26. On a lighter note, an earlier guest at Eglantine Cottage was Thomas Morton, who wrote there his play *Speed the Plough*.

His Mrs Grundy would certainly not have been impressed by the dissolute life of poet Algernon Swinburne, who spent his childhood at East Dene,

Bonchurch. His most extraordinary youthful exploit was climbing Culver Cliff: he was mobbed by nesting seabirds whose 'sudden sound of loud music' brought to mind the Eton chapel organ.

The Old Church, Bonchurch – a place of peace and beauty – has among its graves that of John Stirling, a poet who like Keats died far too young, and who similarly came to the Island in a desperate quest for health. More happily, it was during a short stay at Winterbourne in Bonchurch that Charles Dickens wrote part of *David Copperfield* and every day climbed, with his usual great energy, St Boniface Down – 'it makes a great difference in the climate to get a blow there and come down again'. It was also at Bonchurch that Thomas Macaulay spent the summer of 1850 working on his *History of England*.

Tennyson at Farringford

Alfred Tennyson first rented Farringford in 1853 and bought the house in 1858. The Island inspired some of his greatest poems. *The Charge of the Light Brigade* was written on the Down that now bears his name, *Enoch Arden* and *Maud* in his little summerhouse – now obliterated – within sight of Freshwater Bay.

Farringford was also a perfect place, despite or perhaps because of its remoteness, to receive visits from friends and celebrities, the most unexpected of whom was Prince Albert. It was to Albert that Tennyson was to dedicate his *Idylls of the King* – also mainly written at Farringford – and create Arthur in his likeness, 'scarce other than my own ideal knight'.

The photographer, Julia Margaret Cameron, lived down the road at Dimbola and her eccentricity dwarfed even Tennyson's. When the Italian freedom fighter Garibaldi visited Farringford, he mistook Mrs Cameron – kneeling in supplication that she might take his photograph – for a beggar. Mrs Cameron's apocryphal reply was 'This is not dirt but art!'

Farringford was itself a kind of artistic melting-pot. Sir John Millais discussed painting with Tennyson, but did not convince him of the merits of the Pre-Raphaelite school; Edward Lear played the piano; Sir Arthur Sullivan came down to discuss how to set Tennyson's poetry to music. Alfred conversed with Benjamin Jowett about philosophy, with F D Maurice about theology, with Granville Bradley about geology, which led to many field trips to Alum Bay. Charles Darwin was less impressed; he described his nine-week stay in Freshwater as 'my nine week horrid interruption of all work'.

One of Tennyson's closest friends was Sir John Simeon, the jovial fox-hunting squire from Swainston, whose death occasioned one of his greatest poems, 'In the Garden at Swainston', written there under the shade of a cedar.

West Wight was, however, also a place of great happiness for the poet; he would study the stars from a telescope conveniently situated on Farringford's roof, or mow the lawn by moonlight, or push his wife, Emily, in her wheelchair at great speed over the bridge he had constructed at the back of the house to connect with the Wilderness on the other side of the lane.

Eventually the Tennysons had a summer retreat built on the mainland, at Aldworth, and only came back to Freshwater in the winter, when they would be undisturbed. It was on one of his last crossings of the Solent, on the ferry from

Lymington to Yarmouth, that the poet jotted down some stanzas on an old envelope, and copied them out in his study at Farringford. His nurse came to light the candles, and Alfred recited this newly composed poem to her:

> Sunset and evening star,
>   And one clear call for me.
> And may there be no moaning of the bar,
>   When I put out to sea.

'Crossing the Bar' is both a description of the strange tidal patterns, and wonderful sense of quietude, of the western edge of the Solent and a prefiguration of Tennyson's death.

Emily survived her husband by four years and she is buried in the peaceful cemetery of All Saints' Church, Freshwater, overlooking the estuary of the River Yar and overlooked by the large stone monument made in her husband's memory and erected at the highest point of Tennyson Down.

Modern times

The late 19th century saw a vast influx of tourists and holiday villas, the grandest being Osborne House. Completely redesigned by Prince Albert, as was the nearby Whippingham Church, Osborne became Queen Victoria's place of solace and retirement; Disraeli and John Brown came to pay their compliments, Marconi – who transmitted the first wireless broadcast in 1897 from The Needles Hotel – rigged up a radio link with her errant son Bertie, moored in Osborne Bay. Victoria made her last Solent crossing in 1901, on the royal yacht *Alberta*, in her coffin.

The sea has always exerted a perennial fascination. Uffa Fox – who, as well as his exploits as a balladeer, designed and built many famous boats, including the *Britannia* in which John

Left: Alfred, Lord Tennyson greeting the Italian freedom fighter, Garibaldi, at the poet's beloved Farringford House, Freshwater in 1864.
Below: a study of Tennyson a quarter of a century later in his 80th year. Main picture: the poet's ivy-clad study at Farringford

J B Priestley with his family at their 16th-century country house, Billingham Manor, in the summer of 1933

Ridgeway rowed the Atlantic single-handed – spent most of his life at Cowes, and is buried at Whippingham. Barnes Wallis, inventor of the 'bouncing bomb', was an apprentice at J Samuel White. The designer of the hovercraft, Sir Christopher Cockerell, spent two years on the Island, developing his prototype.

One particular victim of fortune was Prince Louis of Battenburg, who was forced to resign as First Sea Lord shortly before the outbreak of World War I because of his Germanic connections. Prince Louis retired to Kent House in East Cowes. His son, also called Prince Louis, attended Osborne Naval School and went on to become the last Viceroy of India under a more familiar name, Earl Mountbatten. He returned to the Island in 1965, when he was installed as Governor by the Queen.

The Isle of Wight continues to attract those in search of (temporary) tranquillity. Karl Marx, who made three visits to Ryde and Ventnor for the sake of his health, described it in a letter to Engels as 'a little paradise'. George Eliot declared 'the place is perfect . . . in its combination of luxuriant greenth with the delights of a sandy beach'.

Charles Dodgson stayed at Sandown for three idyllic summers; he made friends with a young girl called Gertrude Chataway, whom he entertained with endless stories. One of these found its way into print, under his pen name Lewis Carroll, as *The Hunting of the Snark*.

There must be something inspirational in the waters of South Wight; the Russian novelist Turgenev began the first draft of *Fathers and Sons* while bathing at Ventnor cove. D H Lawrence's novel *The Trespasser* similarly drew on a magical summer he had spent at Freshwater in 1909, as well as on the true story of Helen Corke and a doomed, adulterous affair.

Two refugees from horror were A A Milne and Robert Graves, invalided out from the trenches of World War I to recuperate in the leafy surrounds of Osborne House. As described in *Goodbye To All That*, Graves founded a spoof society in honour of Prince Albert, and found spiritual solace from the monks at Quarr.

Yet there is a darker side to this vision of an earthly paradise. In Alfred Noyes's *No Other Man*, young Mark Adams comes ashore on a Wight –

and a world – populated by the dead. Conversely, John Wyndham's sinister *The Day of the Triffids* ends on an Island fortuitously unaffected by a mutation of the plant kingdom, gone to seed. The Solent acts as a *cordon sanitaire*. Darkest of all is Edward Upward's short story *The Island*, which turns from holiday fun to foreboding, and becomes a Marxist vision of a finer world, an island 'fit for men and women, as it must be, as it will be'. Upward lodged at a staid guesthouse in Freshwater in the 1920s, with his two great friends W H Auden – whose eccentric hat, like Tennyson's before him, caused a great sensation in the village – and Christopher Isherwood, whose autobiography *Lions and Shadows* encapsulates this period.

It was a time for the breaking of icons. Virginia Woolf satirised the holies of Farringford in her drama *Freshwater*. The budding filmstar David Niven was living in Seaview before his assault on Hollywood, John Betjeman was – in his gentle way – parodying Victorian verse forms while acting as a champion for the derided architecture of that lost Age.

Soon, however, another World War was to disrupt the quiet of Island life. It was during the dark days of 1940 that J B Priestley – his home near Godshill, Billingham Manor, requisitioned by the army – began to broadcast his radio 'Postscripts', written to bolster the spirit of a beleaguered nation. In 1948, Priestley moved to Brook Hill House, and now became known as 'Jolly Jack'. A J P Taylor's recollections of the social gatherings there hint at another reason why the Island attracts so many visitors and subsequent residents: the sheer conviviality of the place, a haven of rest and culture set amongst scenery which can suddenly remind one how fragile such comforts are.

Brook Hill House faces Farringford across the waters of Freshwater Bay and the winding ribbon of the Military Road, the favourite haunts of two crusty old literary lions whose spirits can be felt there still.

The Isle of Wight remains a place magically set apart, welcoming yet private, reinvigorating the present with memories of the past. The circle is unbroken.

Brian Hinton is a poet, the Librarian of Freshwater Library and Chairman of the Farringford Tennyson Society.

Sailing for Pleasure, Racing to Win

Crossing to the Isle of Wight on any ferry at the weekend, a first-time visitor to the Solent area cannot help but notice yachts. They are everywhere: skimming along in a stiff breeze, or chugging under engine in a calm. If sailing is new to you, but interesting, you may notice that the yachts are either zig-zagging against the wind, heeling over at the angle beloved by photographers, or spreading out their sails like wings to 'run free'. Although most cruising and racing yachts have engines, in the Solent wise skippers use the tide to help them if possible.

You may also notice that the ferry, a working ship, expects all these leisure boats to keep out of her way. Steam no longer gives way to sail – not leisure sail, anyway. Yachts can be fined for 'obstructing' large vessels 'restricted in their ability to manoeuvre in narrow channels'. You can readily understand this when you watch a giant container ship coming slowly down from Southampton. A small yacht is not even visible when dead ahead. The ship's high bow restricts the view from her bridge. For a small-boat skipper, keeping a sharp look-out and obeying the international regulations for preventing collisions at sea are essential.

First adventures in cruising

The less experienced amateur sailors appreciate the sheltered but tricky waters of the Solent. Here they can set out on a Saturday from a mainland marina in their new boat (ideally armed with sailing school experience) and reach Cowes and other attractive berths up the River Medina, or Yarmouth, both easy to enter at any state of the tide. There they can enjoy a meal ashore in a 'foreign' port, and sail back next day feeling like Columbus at least! Once these modest goals have been achieved, the next step is to master simple chartwork and pilotage. Bembridge, Wootton Creek and the protected peace of Newtown River can be tackled in good weather on a rising tide.

Families or groups of friends can swim, fish, explore in the inflatable dinghy (non-swimmers in life jackets), and pick up milk and bread in friendly Island shops. If they have come to a rally organised by a club or an association of owners of one kind of boat, they may 'raft up' for a party, or have a barbecue ashore. If it rains, it is a pity, but most boat-owners invest in good wet-weather gear.

Boardsailing

This is a comparatively new phenomenon: boards are easily car-topped to the Island, where enthusiasts can always find a sheltered bay whichever way the wind is blowing. Experienced boardsailors, like 1986 Women's World Champion Penny Andrews (née Waye) who lives in Gurnard, race in all weathers, but the Inshore Rescue organisation says: If you're new to the sport, stay in sheltered bays. **Buy a tide-table and learn how**

The earliest mid-18th-century Island regattas featured working fishing craft such as these off Cowes. Inset: a modern yacht passes St Catherine's Point

to use it. Areas like Hurst Narrows, the channel out of the Solent in West Wight, are no place for a novice with a spring ebb running.

Cruising

Although many owners of small boats are content to potter in the Solent and along the coast to Poole or Chichester, many others learn navigation at evening class, and gradually extend their range, achieving longer and longer distances. Isle of Wight harbours act as staging posts for yachts on passage to the east coast or the west country, and for Continental neighbours exploring the south coast. Some cruising yachts now sail from America before the hurricane season, winter in Cowes, then wander on to Scandinavia or the Mediterranean.

The first yacht club

Protected by improved naval and shore defences, in two centuries Cowes grew from the fishing village where Henry VIII built two forts to guard the River Medina, into a busy port with a Post Office specifically to receive mail brought by merchant ships, a Crown Agent, a Customs House and, by 1820, an American consul. Renowned for its beautiful setting and busy shipping, it was also a fashionable resort for sea bathing. It is not surprising that it became the gathering place of keen yachtsmen.

In 1815, they formed themselves into the first true Yacht Club, slowly developed organised yacht racing, and rudimentary handicapping, the ancestor of successive, controversial systems. Royal patronage from George IV and William IV (brought up to sail a miniature ship on Virginia Water) established the Club first as Royal, and then as the Royal Yacht Squadron with special links with the Royal Navy. Most yacht clubs adopted their system of government by Commodore, Flag Officers, and a voting Committee. By 1858, the Squadron had moved into West Cowes Castle, on the site of the early fort, where its members have influenced leisure sailing to this day.

As interest in organised yacht racing spread, more yacht clubs were founded, including the Royal Victoria at Ryde in 1845 (said to be the Queen's answer to the male exclusiveness of the RYS), the Solent (later Royal) at Yarmouth in 1878, Bembridge Sailing Club in 1866, the Island Sailing Club, Cowes, in 1889, and Seaview Yacht Club in 1893.

The Golden Age

From 1882 until the outbreak of World War I, Cowes and Ryde Weeks attracted European royalty and many of the prominent political and social leaders of the day. Self-made millionaires were often refused membership of the Squadron, which remained exclusive.

Many owners kept a yacht to be fashionable, and built larger ones to outshine their rivals, but knew nothing about them. Hence the famous remark of a noble lord (in reply to his professional skipper's 'Will you take the helm, my lord?'): 'Thank you, I never take anything between meals.' (Vivid and very funny, Anthony Heckstall Smith's *Sacred Cowes* is full of good stories about this period.)

Small boat sailing and cruising

From the 1890s, yacht design changed to faster, lighter and beamier boats, and fleets of small, open racing boats (half-raters, one-raters, and so on, designed by Sibbick of Cowes) became accessible to the young and energetic. Cruising in comparatively small yachts was becoming popular too, encouraged by the invigorating example of 'Rob Roy' McGregor, the first to sail single-handed a 21ft yawl (designed for him by Mr John White of Cowes) to a British Regatta on the Seine in 1867.

The America's Cup and the Isle of Wight

In 1851, the year of the Great Exhibition, Commodore Stevens of the New York Yacht Club, the first club of its kind in the United States, arrived in Cowes by invitation to race his schooner *America* against members of the Royal Yacht Squadron. Amused patronage changed to shocked amazement when *America* won the £100 Club Cup for a race round the Island. Apparently, due to a misunderstanding, she sailed a shorter but perfectly legal course, and was indisputably faster than the English yachts. Commodore Stevens therefore carried the ornate trophy back to the New York YC, who resisted over 100 years of British effort to win it back, only to lose to Australia in 1983.

The 1920s and 1930s

After World War I, the ostentatious displays of Cowes and Ryde Weeks declined, but a group of 'big boats', including the famous and successful *Britannia*, inherited by King George V from his father, carried on the traditions of racing in the Solent. As a result of renewed attempts, first by Sir Thomas Lipton with his *Shamrocks*, and then by Sir Thomas Sopwith, the aircraft pioneer, with his two famous *Endeavours*, to win back the America's Cup, the giant 'J' Class yachts evolved on both sides of the Atlantic.

Visitors may be lucky enough to see a restored 'J', *Velsheda*, sailing in the Solent with a crew of enthusiasts who, for a fee, can relive the thrill and power of these huge yachts. *Endeavour I* has also been restored, and may one day race against *Velsheda*.

Cruising in small yachts and dinghy racing began to create a mass, popular sport in the Solent. East Cowes SC had been founded in 1912, and the Island SC in West Cowes raced its own One-Design dinghies. Sailing canoes and a whole string of fast, planing dinghies were also being designed, built and raced by the legendary Uffa Fox, the charismatic Cowes figure who produced so many revolutionary boats and wrote so many interesting books about the contemporary yachting scene that his influence continues to be felt to this day. Specialised day-racing yachts like the

Top: the huge 'J' Class Velsheda *as she was originally in the 1930s and (below) as she is, in her restored form, today. Left: another splendid old 'J', the* Britannia, *once owned with great affection by King George V*

Redwing (1896), the *Mermaid* (1922), the *Solent Sunbeam* (1923) and the *X boat* (1908) were racing regularly then as now, and Yarmouth and Bembridge scows and Seaview One-Design dinghies built in the 1930s are still treasured and raced.

The beginnings of ocean racing

The Americans started first, in 1906, with the

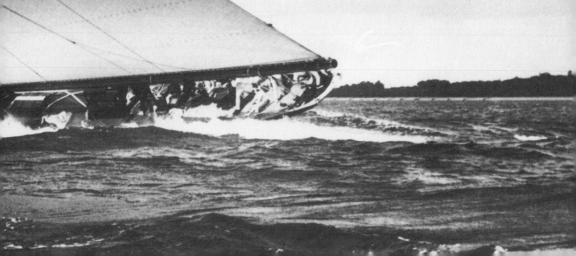

New York–Bermuda Race. Britain was next, with the Fastnet, first sailed in 1925, over a 605-mile course from Ryde, out round the Fastnet Rock off the southern coast of Ireland, and back to Plymouth. Other classic offshore races were added, the first being the Channel Race, from Cowes, round the Royal Sovereign light vessel, to Cherbourg, and back to Cowes. The Ocean Racing Club (later Royal) was formed to manage and augment them, and membership is now based on completing a Fastnet, and two other offshore races.

Racing today
The technology learned in World War II was soon adapted to the racing and cruising yachts of the 1950s and 1960s. Moulded GRP (fibreglass) construction, aluminium masts and nylon sails reduced maintenance costs, so traditional building in wood gradually died out except in specialist yards. Famous Cowes-based yachtsmen of the 1960s and 1970s – Sir Max Aitken, founder of the Earls Court Boatshow, and the Rt Hon Edward Heath, MBE, first and only Prime Minister to captain an Admiral's Cup team – had boats designed and built in Cowes by Souters and Claire Lallow. These top yachts of their day foreshadowed the revolution in design and technology which was to produce the ultra-light, 'stripped-out' racer of the 1980s, with inevitable effects on the design of cruising yachts. Some critics do not view this as a change for the better.

Modern ocean racing
In 1957 the RORC instituted the Admiral's Cup (presented by Sir Miles Wyatt, honorary 'Admiral' of the Club at that time) to attract foreign racing yachts to Cowes Week, now always held in

the first week of August. It has become a World Team Championship, competed for every odd-numbered year, by three 'top yachts' from 18 or so countries, and include three inshore races, the RORC Channel Race, and of course, the Fastnet. Britain has won the Cup in eight out of 20 contests. Visitors can either watch the 10am start of the Fastnet from the Esplanade west of the Royal Yacht Squadron, or picnic on the cliffs above The Needles and watch the fleet coming out through Hurst Narrows.

The Round the World Race for maxi-yachts (Simon Le Bon's *Drum*, for example) grew out of the attempt of a Portsmouth greengrocer, Alec Rose, to beat RYS member Sir Francis Chichester's time in *Gypsy Moth IV* when he pioneered a single-handed circumnavigation of the world. It was a sign of changed times that a newly knighted Sir Alec Rose was elected to the Squadron on his triumphant return in *Lively Lady*. The race starts from Portsmouth, through the Solent, in September every fourth year (next one: 1989/90). Sir Francis had previously helped to organise, and then won, the first single-handed transatlantic race in 1960.

The Round the Island Race – Cowes to Cowes
RIR for short, the largest yacht race in the world has been run by the Island Sailing Club on a Saturday, every June (date according to tide) since originator Cyril Windeler offered a replica of a gold Roman bowl as the winner's Challenge Cup in 1931. From modest beginnings, the race now attracts over 1,200 starters. Organised in Divisions for the true racers, and Classes for the cruisers enjoying their annual turn-out, yacht clubs and sailing associations run their own championships under the RIR umbrella, and the whole thing works with the help of a bank of computers and an army of Club volunteers. Multihulls now naturally capture the fastest time record (3hrs 59mins in 1986) but they are excluded from the historic major prizes reserved for monohulls – usually won now by top racing yachts, including Edward Heath's *Morning Cloud* four times. Watch the start – very early – at Cowes, or choose The Needles, the downland area to the east of Freshwater, St Catherines, or Culver Cliff for a panoramic view of 1,200 vivid spinnakers stretching right along 'the back of the Island' if wind and weather are right. Ring the Island Sailing Club for the day and time on (0983) 296621.

Just one of the dramatic sights during Cowes Week: Tigre racing to win, with chute and spinnaker billowing

Jean Cook is a freelance yachting journalist, who, with her husband, Dennis, edits the Island Sailing Club magazine, and writes a column in the Isle of Wight County Press.

ISLE OF WIGHT

Gazetteer

Each entry in this Gazetteer has the atlas
page number on which the place can be
found and its National Grid reference
included under the heading.
An explanation of how to use the National
Grid is given on page 80.

Above: decorative ironwork porch at Cowes

Alum Bay and The Needles

Map Ref: 86SZ3085

Imagine a vast right-angled bay, with one arm a stark and dramatic wall of white cliff plunging straight into the sea and stretching westward to the famous chalk stacks of The Needles. In contrast, the other arm presents crumbling tawny cliffs, a gentle coast, composed of the almost equally famous Alum Bay coloured sands, 20 or more different shades showing up brightest after rain. (Do not be tempted to climb after them, however, because these cliffs can give way at any time.) You may still

The colourful sweep of Alum Bay and (below) the sand-filled souvenirs sold in the shop on the cliff above

find Victorian landscape pictures on the Island 'painted' with the sands.

The sands, and shapes that can be filled with them, are sold on the cliffs above in The Needles Pleasure Park, which also offers an amusement centre and playground, working pottery, model railway, bar and café. The studio of Alum Bay Glass is full of colourful hand-blown goblets, vases and jewellery. From the gallery the glass-blowers can be seen at work with their long blowpipes.

On the cliff edge stands a monument to Marconi, who set up The Needles Wireless and Telegraph Station here at the end of the last century and exchanged a pioneer radio message with a tug in the bay below. The park is useful as a communications centre, too. Here you can catch buses inland, ride a chairlift to the beach, book a boat trip to view The Needles and their red and white-banded lighthouse at close quarters, or take a minibus to the remnant of chalk cliffs, an ever-narrowing headland 500ft (152m) above the sea with a breeze off the Atlantic and gulls wheeling below. An exhilarating roof-of-the-world walk leads to The Needles Battery, a recently restored fort with magnificent views of the bay and the Dorset coast beyond.

Outside the park, the Museum of Clocks has an amazing collection, comprising 'grandfathers', church clocks, musical and mystery clocks and other forms of timekeeping.

Headon Hill, a ridge of sandy heath, offers undemanding walks and attractive picnic spots that overlook the Solent.

Alverstone

Map Ref: 88SZ5785

This hamlet, lying at the back of Sandown, is in the middle of a long stretch of marshland surrounding the Eastern Yar as it wends toward

Wild flowers and lush water plants beside the Yar at Alverstone

Bembridge harbour under the downs. The railway is long closed, but its track remains as stretches of straight footpath on both sides of the road. Alverstone is famous locally for its wild flowers. A path signposted over a stile and through the waterworks, which stands on the site of the old mill, leads to delightful green walks along the river banks, bright with lush water plants in summer.

Arreton

Map Ref: 91SZ5386

Through the wide vale of Arreton the village rambles along the main road, but its ancient heart lies behind the White Lion pub. A church stood here 1200 years ago; the monks of Quarr Abbey rebuilt it together with a farmhouse and a great tithe barn, and here it all lies, bowered in trees. The church is massively buttressed and has a squat tower as if built partly as a fortress, but inside all is light and space with many treasures, including a brass that commemorates one Harry Hawles who fought at Agincourt in 1415. Outside stands the grave of 'The Dairyman's Daughter', heroine of a tract popular in Victorian times and still in print.

The oldest rooms in Arreton

Island in Trust

The National Trust became involved in the Isle of Wight in 1922 when it was given St Boniface Down, behind Ventnor, to be enjoyed by the public in perpetuity. The Trust now cares for over 3,000 acres of land, most of it freely open to visitors, which offers some of the best landscape on the Island. It owns no country houses, but The Needles Battery, the Old Town Hall at Newtown, and Bembridge Windmill are open at a charge at published times.

To explore the Trust's Island properties, start at the western end, where the walk up to The Needles headland from Alum Bay offers the first sight of the famous sea-stacks lined out towards Purbeck and the Dorset coasts. They represent the still-receding remains of the line of chalk hill and sea cliffs that stretched across what is now Christchurch Bay, before the steadily rising sea levels after the last Ice Age gave birth to the Island some 8,000 years ago.

On the headland, The Needles Battery, built in 1863, was part of Lord Palmerston's plans to defend Portsmouth naval base and to deter any ideas of military enterprise on the part of Napoleon III.

Eastwards, the downs and cliffs run to Freshwater Bay over closely sheep-cropped turf up to Tennyson Down and the granite memorial to Queen Victoria's favourite poet laureate. He loved these downs and for many years lived at Farringford, just below.

Beyond Freshwater Bay the track over Afton Down and its golf course leads on up to the summit of Brook Down, crowned with a group of Bronze Age round barrows commanding views that, in some respects, have remained unaltered since these ancient burial mounds were created 3,500 years ago. Here also flourish in profusion the plants, butterflies and other creatures that are so characteristic of well-grazed downland.

Below the downs, crumbling sea-cliffs of many-coloured sandstones and clays shelter the bathing beaches of Compton Bay and provide plants to feed almost the only British colony of Glanville fritillary butterflies.

At Mottistone, park in the village and walk up the sunken trackways to the Longstone, remains of a Stone Age burial chamber that was already 2,000 years old when the round barrows on the downs were built. Here the Island's first farmers used stone axes to clear the ancient

The granite memorial cross to Tennyson, erected at the highest point on Tennyson Down where the poet loved to walk

forests and began to create the landscapes that we know today.

Six miles to the north is Newtown, its multi-fingered estuary a haven for summer yachtsmen and a vital refuge for thousands of seabirds and wildfowl in winter. Above the harbour, the outline of the medieval village is etched in banks and hedges around flower-rich meadows.

At the Island's southern tip, St Catherine's Down, crowned with its strange medieval lighthouse, provides Island-wide views as a fitting reward for climbing from the Council's viewpoint car park above Blackgang Chine.

Further east the hilltop views from the heather-capped Ventnor Downs and Culver Cliffs are over the great historic shipping lanes and anchorages of Spithead and St Helens roads to the South Downs. But on a good day you can still see The Needles all the way from Ventnor Downs.

John Simpson is the National Trust's Land Agent for the Isle of Wight and South West Hampshire.

Manor incorporate part of the monks' original farmhouse, but the building is mainly Elizabethan with not only a handsome stone front and gracious rooms, but also the ghost of little Annabel, murdered by her brother. There is, in addition, a collection of dolls and dolls' houses and the National Wireless Museum. The manor is open to the public as is the Arreton Country Craft Village nearby, where visitors can watch boat builders, jewellers and candlemakers at work – the collection of crafts varies from year

to year. Beside the craft centre the monks' huge barn stands forlorn and roofless, awaiting repair.

Haseley Manor at the other end of the village is a jumble of styles. It, too, was begun by the monks. A later owner, Dowsabelle Myll, took the Island's governor for her lover and would dance with him from Haseley to the foot of the down. The manor acquired Georgian and Victorian features, but by 1976 it was derelict. Now lovingly restored, it is open to the public, along with the Island's

largest pottery studio in which demonstrations are given on the hour, every hour. There is also a children's play area with a tree house and a herb garden 'with cures for all ailments.'

The Vale of Arreton's fertile red soil is the Island's vegetable basket, with many farms and nurseries putting up 'pick your own' notices in season.

AA recommends:
Guesthouse: Stickworth Hall, *tel.* (0983) 77233

Atherfield

Map Ref: 90SZ4679

Between Shorwell and the sea meander miles of lanes, green-banked but with hardly a hedge. They wind through acres of meadows undulating to the cliff's edge, with wide views of the Channel and the great sweep of downs from St Catherine's Point right round to Freshwater in the west. They pass a few farms, old stone barns and ricks. Atherfield is unspoiled farming country with little traffic, so fine for walking. At dusk, three fence posts in a row may be topped with a trio of little owls, and the larger barn owl might glide out from a rickyard.

Along the seaward side runs the Military Road, a field's width from the cliff edge, which was originally a track built during the 19th century to connect the various fortifications set up in fear of an invasion from France. During the Depression it was surfaced and has become one of the finest scenic roads in England. On some days one can see right across to the downs of Dorset: this means it is going to rain!

It is here that the coastal footpath which rings the Island leads along the edge of the cliff and looks down into the bay that has wrecked so many ships. It can be reached across the fields beside Whale Chine, a way down to the shore through a dramatic, bare-sided fissure in the

Bembridge windmill, built about 1700, is the only windmill to survive on the Island. Inset: fishing boats in Brading Haven, Bembridge harbour

cliffs eroded into ridges and pinnacles by sea winds, and so deep and narrow that it is always cold and shadowed at the bottom. Further along, the Coastal Path passes Atherfield Point and a row of coastguard cottages; there used to be a lifeboat at Atherfield. On either side of a holiday camp, which covers the cliff top for a short space, there are other paths down to the shore. But, although it has a wild beauty of its own, this is no place for bathing. The beach is rough and shingly and the roaring waves have a sinister undertow.

Bembridge

Map Ref: 89SZ6487

Beneath the great green headland of
Culver, Bembridge village sprawls
from wooded harbour to downs,
with many wooded alleys and roads
(with car parks) leading to a vast
sandy shore.

Legend tells of ancient oakwoods
where Druids performed their rites,
until the murder of a Holy Man
brought a retributory flood that
inundated all the land. Here history
begins – at one time the sea
stretched right up to Brading
until the causeway was built in
1878.

Today the small harbour, lined
with old houseboats along one side,
is full of yachts coming and going –
especially Bembridge Redwings with
their bright sails. Visit St Helen's
opposite by the small ferry, or walk
through the reclaimed meadows to
Brading, past the windmill and
Bembridge Airport.

For hundreds of years Bembridge
was a rough fishing hamlet, with
smuggling taking place on the side.
Molly Downer, a smuggling witch,
left her cottage to the vicar who,
much embarrassed, burned it down!
But the Victorians changed all that,
turning the place into a fashionable
resort with large hotels and holiday
villas in their own grounds. Their
railway has gone now, but a large
flourishing village remains with a
street of shops, a spacious church
and a fine maritime museum with a
model of the harbour, showing its
history and pictures of old
horsedrawn lifeboats. At Lane End,
the present lifeboat station, on its
long, long jetty, is sometimes open
to the public. Although fishing is no
longer important here try the
restaurants, such as the Crab and
Lobster at Forelands, for delicious
local shellfish. The Pilot Boat pub,
by the harbour, has decks and
portholes.

Below Culver lies Bembridge
School, founded by John
Whitehouse, who was secretary to
Lloyd George. Passionate about
Ruskin, he collected everything the
art critic wrote. The Ruskin
Collection, consulted by scholars
world-wide, can be visited by
appointment.

A pretty cliff walk leads to
Whitecliff Bay, a fine sandy beach
tucked under the white wall of
Culver Cliff, backed by cafés, a car
park and an Activity Centre. This
offers golf, archery and shooting,
and there is a children's playground
and picnic area.

AA recommends:
Hotels: Birdham, I Steyne Rd, 2-star,
tel. (0983) 872875
Elms Country, 2-star Country House
Hotel, *tel.* (0983) 872248
Highbury, Lane End, 2-star, *tel.* (0983)
872838
Self Catering: Home Cottage (house),
47 Howgate Rd, *tel.* (0983) 403958

*Some of the absorbing exhibits at the
Maritime Museum in Bembridge*

Binstead

Map Ref: 88SZ5792

Like Arreton, Binstead must not be
judged by its main street – in this
case lined with red brick and
thunderous with traffic. To the
south are estates of new housing,
but to the north lies a different
world of quiet lanes shadowed by
old trees, wandering between stone
walls to church and shore.

The Romans discovered the local
outcrops of hard limestone. Later
this was used in the building of
Chichester Cathedral and Beaulieu
Abbey, among others. These leafy
lanes and secluded houses cover the
old pits, the local name 'Quarr'
being derived from 'quarry'.

The original Quarr Abbey,
founded in 1132, was the centre of
life here until its dissolution by
Henry VIII. Now little remains in
the sea meadows but an archway, a
delicate stone window, fragments of
a wall where cows graze and a barn
incorporated into a farmhouse, all
of which can be seen from a
footpath. But the monks returned.
In 1907 a new abbey began to rise,
with tall pointed towers of glowing
Flemish brick adding a touch of
Byzantium to the skyline; a most
striking building. The drive and
chapel are open to all, service times
being posted at the door.

Parts of the parish church date
from Norman times. Today, no-one
would guess that it was half
destroyed by fire in 1969, since
when some interesting stained glass
windows have been added. Past the
church in its tranquil wooded
corner, Ladies Walk leads on to
Ryde, but a turn off beside the
stream leads out on to the beach,
pebbly and muddy certainly, but
with fine views of the Solent and all
its shipping; a good place for picnics
rather than bathing.

Just outside the village, Brickfields
Horsecountry offers a change of
scene, an entertainments centre with
a comfortable bar and restaurant,
carriage rides, blacksmith's
demonstrations, and a children's
'animal encounter' area. Shire
horses and various horsey events in
the international-size indoor arena
can be watched from the restaurant.

Blackgang

Map Ref: 90SZ4876

The hamlet of Blackgang lies on a
ledge above 400ft (122m) cliffs and
below the green slopes of St
Catherine's Down, with its
conspicuous ruined oratory. When
the Holy Man from the oratory met
the cannibal Giant of Chale, says
folklore, he cursed him and his land:

*Nor flower nor fruit this earth shall
bear
And all shall be dark and waste and
bare.*

So a great dark chasm appeared in
the cliffs. The Dabell family first
opened it to the public in 1845.
Queen Victoria paid a visit. Today
there are amusements for every
taste: beautiful water gardens, a
Wild West town, Jungleland,
Nurseryland, Smugglers' Cave,
Dinosaur Park, Crooked House, all
floodlit on summer evenings. For
adults there is a fine collection of
wreck and smuggling pictures, the
story of Blackgang landslips, a
maritime exhibition in St
Catherine's Quay, and a complete
replica of a Victorian water-
powered sawmill, with a forge and
wheelwright's shop. A wonderful
coastal panorama spreads out on
either hand from the Look Out.

*Not all the saws are powered by water
at Blackgang Sawmill Museum*

Even outside the park, the
scenery is spectacular. From the
picnic and viewpoint car park
above, you can see right across the
scalloped bays of the south-west
coast to The Needles and the
Dorset coast beyond.

East of the chine, St Catherine's
breaks off abruptly, ending in a
towering wall of inner cliff looming
above – the high point is Windy
Corner. Beneath it, the road which
was once the main route to Niton,
falls away into a wilderness of
boulders, brambles, streams and
grassy slopes. It was destroyed by a
massive cliff fall in 1928 and goes
on falling, several houses
disappearing in 1978.

Bonchurch

Map Ref: 91SZ5778

In about AD700, a Devon boy entered a Hampshire monastery and was given the name Boniface. Many years later, tradition tells, he came to the Undercliff and established a church, now called after him, as is the down towering above it. For hundreds of years Bonchurch was a fishing and quarrying hamlet, but the last century brought numerous visitors who built their large secluded houses in wooded grounds, while its peace and beauty drew many literary figures.

Today Bonchurch is joined to Ventnor, but manages to maintain its charming, tree-hung identity. There is a row of cottages and a working forge opposite The Pond – a long stretch of water bowered in willow and beech, a haven for mallard and moorhen. The little street is totally sheltered from the north by the huge bulk of St Boniface Down. Further along, a fountain stands under a stone archway and a pyramid is set in the wall, erected in 1773 as a sample of local stone. The quarries are long overgrown, but a road above is called The Pitts. Steep flights of stone steps wind between different terraces of the village.

Here at Winterbourne, now a hotel, Dickens wrote part of *David Copperfield*, Thackeray came to the village for holidays, Macaulay stayed at Madeira Hall. In this century, H de Vere Stacpoole, author of *The Blue Lagoon* lived at Cliff Dene and gave The Pond, then part of his grounds, to the village.

Swinburne, the poet, lived at East Dene as a boy, learning to swim in Monks Bay below. Past the striking Drum Tower entrance to his house, a field path leads to St Boniface church (built about 1070) an austere little building often packed to the door in summer for candlelit evensong. Swinburne's grave lies beside the 'new' church built in the last century, half-way up the hill to Upper Bonchurch.

Shore Road winds steeply down to a car park above a stony beach and a handful of cafés on the seawall where you can buy fresh local seafood.

Brading

Map Ref: 88SZ6086

A long, narrow street of cottages slopes downhill from the Bull Ring, then up again to the hill where St Wilfred once converted the Island's heathen. Today an ancient and

The churchyard of charming 11th-century Old Church of St Boniface contains many interesting graves

beautiful church, marks the spot. It is rich in family tombs, particularly the full-length painted effigies of the Oglander family who lived at nearby Nunwell House from Norman times until 1980. Nunwell, under its hanging beech woods, is open to the public on some days in summer. Henry VIII paid a visit and Charles I came to stay.

Opposite the church stands, reputedly, the oldest house in Wight, its narrow galleries and twisting stairs now occupied by Osborn-Smith's Wax Museum. This traces the history of the Island in animated and finely detailed period tableaux, including Queen Victoria at Osborne. 'Animal World' lies adjacent to the Wax Museum.

Lilliput, the doll museum, also in the High Street, has an Egyptian sandstone exhibit dating from 2000BC and a vast collection including dolls given by Noel Coward and Nikita Krushchev. Close by stands the old Town Hall, part of its ground floor enclosed only by bars – this was the town gaol, complete with whipping post and stocks. Brading has a fascinating collection of historic documents which are exhibited from time to time in the council chamber upstairs.

At the western end, an area called Morton, stands the Island's finest Roman villa with its beautiful mosaic floors. Morton Manor with terraced gardens and elegant Georgian rooms is open in summer.

The Anglers Inn, which now overlooks the narrow River Yar winding through green fields, was once a sailors' and smugglers' pub: before the embankment was built, the sea came right up to the back of the High Street and all the lush meadows were Brading Haven, lined with quays and boats.

Charles I spent his last night of freedom here at Brading's Nunwell House

Carisbrooke Castle

The only medieval castle on the Island, and until 1944 the official residence of the Island Governor, this stands on a spur of chalk downland in the Bowcombe Valley, 1 mile (1.6km) south-west of Newport.

The early Norman castle, itself adapted from a late Saxon defensive structure, was strengthened early in the 12th century by the building of the present stone walls, in which a few of the original cross-shaped archery loopholes can still be found. The occasional discovery, in the ground outside the walls, of the metal arrowheads of crossbow bolts fired from the castle is evidence of former sieges, particularly during the wars with France in the 14th century.

The castle was never taken by storm, although it was captured once, during its first siege in 1136. The then owner, Baldwin de Redvers, who was supporting the Empress Matilda, prepared to defend his newly fortified castle against King Stephen, and provisioned it for an extended siege. A sudden drought caused the wells to run dry, however, and the castle was soon surrendered.

There are two medieval wells in the castle. One is reached by climbing the 71 steps up to the massive shell-keep. The well shaft is 160ft (49m) deep, but the first 53ft (16m) are accounted for by the height of the artificial mound on which the keep tower stands. This well is unreliable and usually dry.

The other well, in the middle of the castle courtyard, is 161ft (49m) deep and manages to touch the

Top: Carisbrooke Castle is given an ominous look by this early print

Above: on a circular tour of the Castle's 16th-century Donkey Well

course of an underground stream, which keeps the water level fairly stable. Although the well is medieval, the present well-house and winding wheel date to the 1580s; and for several centuries the wheel has been powered by donkeys. The donkey is trained to walk until it sees the shackle of the bucket appearing out of the well shaft. Today the bucket is lowered only a token distance, and a team of donkeys shares the work.

The two drum towers flanking the gatehouse tell their own story of evolving medieval warfare. At the lower levels are archery loopholes, but higher up are openings of a different shape – like inverted keyholds – and these, dating to the late 14th century, are for early handguns. The continuing evolution of

cannon, however, threatened to make the medieval walls obsolete; and with the continuing threat of Spanish invasion in the 1590s, the whole castle was enclosed by an impressive system of artillery fortifications, nearly a mile in circuit.

William the Conqueror made a visit to the castle in 1082, but the most famous royal connection is with Charles I, who was a prisoner at Carisbrooke from November 1647 to September 1648. His morning exercise was the walk round the battlements, which can still be enjoyed by visitors today. A window through which he made an unsuccessful escape attempt can still be seen in the north curtain wall near the postern gate.

Jack Jones

Brighstone

Map Ref: 87SZ4282

A row of pretty thatched cottages, the tea gardens and church form the heart of old Brighstone. Older still is the nearby hamlet of Limerstone where the Tichborne family founded a priory; some of its stones are used in the present farmhouse.

The pub is called the Three Bishops, commemorating first of all Bishop Ken who wrote the famous hymns 'Awake my soul and with the sun' and 'Glory to thee my God this night'. While pacing the rectory gardens, Samuel Wilberforce, later a bishop, used to entertain his father, William, famous for his anti-slavery campaign. The walk along the top of the down above is named after him. The third bishop, Doctor Moberley, was headmaster of Winchester College before changing career. There is a monument to the three men in the church which dates in part from the 14th century. In the churchyard are the graves of Moses Munt and Thomas Cotton, both drowned when the Brighstone lifeboat capsized at the wreck of the *Sirenia* in 1888.

White cliffs and weathered rocks at Brook, looking towards the high sweep of Tennyson Down

The picturesque post office and cottages at North Street, Brighstone

Brighstone is an excellent centre for walkers exploring West Wight. A path through fields leads to Grange Chine and the wild and beautiful shore, with miles of sand and rock ledges. The monks of Quarr once had a barn or grange here. Other paths lead up to Wilberforce's Walk and the high chalk downs beyond. A lane beside the church dips down to the picturesque old thatched and stone-mullioned farmhouse Waytescourt, once seat of the Wayte family who owned most of the village.

Hunnyhill Dairy Farm is open to the public in summer. Watch the cows being milked or visit pigs, horses, sheep and poultry. There are tractor rides, cream teas and facilities for the disabled.

Brook

Map Ref: 87SZ3883

Tree-hung inland, bare on the cliffs, the village straggles from the downs to the sea. Brook Hill House, a mansion built high on the hill above, was once the home of J B Priestley, although in World War I the Germans had it marked on their invasion maps as a fort.

The stone wall down one side of the road once enclosed the grounds of the manor, Brook House, owned by the Seely family – great benefactors to the neighbourhood. It built schools, libraries and the Seely Hall in Brook, where the Island's Natural History Society stages an exhibition every year for the month of August. Visitors are shown the amazing variety of birds and flowers, as well as the walks and nature trails to be found on the Island – it is called Local Look.

Up towards the downs, the small church stands on a little knoll bright with daffodils in spring. It was built in 1862 to replace an earlier building destroyed by fire, with some of the original stone being re-used in the churchyard wall. Inside hang the lifeboat boards, an impressive list of all the wrecks attended. Down on the cliffs stands the lifeboat house.

There is a car park for the beach here, another at Hanover Point further west and one more at Compton Chine. Each is beside a pathway down to the shore through crumbly yellow-brown cliffs, whose sea-washed rocks and ledges were so rich in fossils that dinosaur bones were commonly used in the village as doorsteps. Close to the cliffs stands Hanover House, partly Elizabethan, which is now a restaurant and tea garden.

Calbourne

Map Ref: 87SZ4286

A green sloping down from an ancient church, the pump under its conical roof, a white manor house glimpsed across the lake through tall beech trees – Calbourne is one of the most beautiful, unspoilt villages on the Island. King Egbert granted land for the church in AD826. The tower was struck by lightning in 1683; a stone on it reads: 'I am risen from ye ruins of near seventy years.'

A flint-built lodge marks the entrance to Westover, the manor (not open) where ducks nest by the lake and Jacob sheep graze spacious parkland. Beside the lodge lies Winkle Street, a row of thatched cottages opposite the stream, much visited and photographed. Winkle in this case means cul-de-sac. The Caul Bourne (or stream) which names the village, once powered five mills on its way north.

Upper Calbourne Mill, first mentioned in 1299, is open to the public and its complex machinery can still grind into action as the 20ft (6m) water wheel begins to turn. The millpond and a stretch of the stream have been turned into a charming water garden with seats along the flowery banks, and there are many water fowl.

A little further west, Chessell Pottery is housed in a 300-year-old barn. The porcelain bowls and vases contain delicate and intricate forms

Just two of the fascinating exhibits that can be seen at Calbourne Mill

inspired by rock pools and coral – visitors can watch them being made. Calbourne is traditionally a craft centre. Where the garage now stands at the crossroads, great wagons were made; their wheels were as high as a man, and it took five cart horses to draw them.

To the east of the village lies Swainston Manor, now a residential hotel that owes its name to one Swein, leader of the Danish invaders who raided West Wight in AD1001. Later, the Bishop of Winchester built himself a hall here. Rebuilt in the 18th century, it was gutted during World War II by incendiary bombs, but since being carefully restored it makes an elegant picture among its acres of green parkland where Tennyson, visiting his friends the Simeons, was inspired to write his long operatic poem, *Maud*.

Carisbrooke

Map Ref: 84SZ4888

The village winds steeply upward between the castle on its hill to the south and the church on its ledge high above the street. Carisbrooke

Winkle Street in Calbourne, possibly the Island's most beautiful village

Priory was suppressed in the 15th century, but the monks' church remains, a majestic building with a soaring tower and a fine peal of eight bells. Inside there are massive Norman pillars, a now-blocked doorway (through which the monks once entered) and the beautiful angel tomb of Lady Wadham, Jane Seymour's aunt. Outside stands a

A bird's-eye view of Carisbrooke village and its majestic church

yew tree older than any of the lichened monuments beside it.

The High Street is a mixture of old and new, and includes an Italian restaurant, an antiques shop and a working pottery housed in a 16th-century pub with a tea garden attached. Beside it is the most picturesque part of the village. This is Castle Street – a lane of old cottages leading to a ford and a footpath by the stream with a good view of the castle above. Beyond, there are pleasant walks along the Lukely Brook, up through a steep meadow to the castle, or round the castle's green moats.

The Lukely Brook once served at least six mills. Kents Mill has recently been rescued from ruin and tons of silt dredged to restore the pond to its original state.

The next mill downstream, Priory, has disappeared completely, its site being taken over by the waterworks. Since this became redundant the Water Board has opened its ground to the public, free. Tucked away behind the house lies a quiet lake, the old mill pond, beloved of ducks, with seats for picnics on the wide grass banks. Look for the entrance where the brook flows out beside the road.

North of the village, but joined to it, lies Gunville, on land reclaimed from Parkhurst Forest. This is an area consisting of mostly red brick with a few large warehouse-shops and a garden centre.

Chale

Map Ref: 90SZ4877

Very old, called Cela in the Domesday Book, the village is shaped like a dumb-bell. Houses clustering round a large inland green are connected by Chale Street – a mile-long straggle of cottages – to the main settlement on the cliffs – 'main' because here are a church, school and post office. The whole area is agricultural and although there is no way down the cliffs to the beach, fine walking is possible along the cliff-tops up to St Catherine's Down, where the alarm beacon once flared its warning at the sighting of the Spanish Armada.

Rugged St Andrew's Church was begun in 1114, and even the tower has withstood five centuries of Channel gales on this exposed site. From the churchyard there is a fine view of the wild coast westward and even on a calm day the air carries the growling thunder of waves below. Among many sailors' graves are monuments to those aboard the *Clarendon*. She was wrecked close by in 1836, pounded to pieces on the rocks in a few minutes. Next to the church was a small pub called The White Mouse: with timber thrown ashore from the wreck, it was enlarged and renamed The Clarendon. Today it offers an

A telephone box adds a splash of red to the green at ancient Chale

Osborne House

In September 1846 Queen Victoria wrote: 'It seems to me like a dream to be here now in our house, of which we laid the stone 15 months ago.' It was 15 September when she, with Prince Albert and their four children, walked the few yards from old Osborne House into the Pavilion, the first completed wing of their new home. It was indeed their own home, paid for with their own money and designed by Prince Albert, with practical advice from his builder-contractor Thomas Cubitt. Osborne was designed to fit a landscape. Prince Albert saw in the Solent a resemblance to the Bay of Naples and he visualised an Italian villa looking over terraced gardens and green lawns to the blue waters of Osborne Bay. The Flag Tower soaring above the Pavilion came into use as soon as the family moved in. From here Prince Albert supervised the grading and planting of the terraces, using signal flags to direct the workmen. It was work he loved, and today we enjoy the mature results of his gardening and tree planting.

In the Pavilion the formal rooms were the drawing room, billiard room and dining room. The first two were unusually close together, separated only by pillars of imitation marble. Similar pillars divided the long drawing room, so that the two rooms were also united by a similarity of style. The drawing room was intended to include works of art, and the life-size marble statues of the Queen's four oldest children, representing the seasons, are prominent among all the gilded furniture. The dining room was furnished in a heavier, solemn style, including a massive sideboard in mahogany. This came into its own at Christmas when it supported an equally massive baron of beef which could weigh about 250lb (113kg).

In contrast, the private apartments on the first floor have a cosy, cluttered appearance, with overblown roses woven into the carpet, balloon-backed chairs, and chintz curtains at the window. In Queen Victoria's dressing room we can see the Christmas present which Prince Albert gave her in 1853, a dressing glass and toilet service by Mintons, with little cherubs playing round the oval mirror. Next door is the bedroom with its high-testered bed where the Queen died on 22 January 1901. By this time the family house had long since grown in size, first with the completion of the Household Wing in 1851 and then in 1890 by the addition of the Durbar Room. From 1854 there was also the Swiss Cottage where the children's education was widened through Prince Albert's interest in modern educational theories. Here they cooked, sewed, learned carpentry and gardened – paid by their father the market price for the crops. 'Dear modest, unpretentious Osborne' had become what the royal couple had intended, a happy family home.

Johanas Jones is a part-time history lecturer for the Department of Adult Education at Southampton University

An 1880 engraving showing the east front of Osborne House, East Cowes

Above: Osborne House dining room where Victoria lay in state in 1901

The churchyard at St Andrews, Chale has several table tombs and the graves of many sailors, including those who perished in the infamous Clarendon *shipwreck in 1836*

interesting selection of pub food, with music every night in the bar. Coming full circle, its extension is called The White Mouse.

AA recommends:
Hotels: Clarendon Hotel & Wight Mouse Inn, I-star, *tel.* (0983) 730431

Chillerton

Map Ref: 90SZ4984

A long, rambling village lining a deep fold in the downs, Chillerton appears more new than old, though Sheat Manor has a fine E-shaped south front (E for the Monarch, Elizabeth I). It shares a church with Gatcombe, which can be reached in a pleasant half-mile walk through woods and fields after crossing the stream near the manor. It is a centre for various downland walks, one along the western ridge revealing ancient and modern side by side: Iron Age fort alongside television mast.

The road climbs to the south, passing the fine old stone barns of Chillerton Farm, then plunges down by Billingham Manor, reputedly much haunted. The head of Charles I was said to appear every time an execution was carried out at Parkhurst Prison.

Colwell

Map Ref: 86SZ3288

Today, Colwell Common is a vast green area with a few seats. Soldiers camped here when Napoleon's invasion was feared: later it was a favourite site for Gypsy camps. Apart from a few cottages, most of Colwell hamlet is fairly recent, built as support to the forts or the holiday trade. Behind the green a road leads down to a sheltered Solent beach with wide seawalls and the remains of a jetty specially built to land the heavy guns for The Needles Battery. Here at Colwell Chine there is a large car park, beach cafés and boat trips round the bay in summer.

AA recommends:
Self Catering: Solent Court Holiday Apartments (flats), Colwell Chine Rd, *tel.* (0983) 754515

Cowes – East

Map Ref: 84SZ5095

A pair of huge doors, together painted to form the Union Jack, make a landmark right across Cowes; this was painted by the factory owner, British Hovercraft, to celebrate the Queen's Silver Jubilee and retained by popular vote. East Cowes is an industrial centre and terminus for the car ferry to Southampton. There is a short promenade with fine views of

the mouth of the River Medina, and the harbour with all its sea traffic. The Floating Bridge, a chain ferry, takes passengers and vehicles across the Medina to West Cowes.

Not a hovercraft but the chain ferry linking East and West Cowes

Behind the factories and boat-yards is the different world of mock-medieval Norris Castle, lying battlemented and towered among lawns and old trees. It was built by the architect James Wyatt in about 1805 and is very important in the Island's history, for it was here that Princess Victoria came to stay, and tasted the freedom of shore and country. As Queen Victoria she wanted to buy the castle, but when this proved impossible she chose Osborne, next door.

Norris Castle is no longer open to the public, but school visits may be made in summer. Inside, it is rich in antique furniture and its apartments include Princess Victoria's bedroom.

Cowes – West

Map Ref: 84SZ4995

Cowes is probably the most famous place on Wight, thanks to its annual international yachting festival, known simply as Cowes Week. A mere huddle of fishermen's shacks at the mouth of the Medina until Henry VIII's reign, it grew into a village round West Cowe, the coastal fort he ordered to be built.

Today, long narrow High Street curves along the west front, hiding the sea. At its western end, Watch House Lane (named after the Customs House) leads down to the Parade, a wide square fronting the Solent. A plaque on the shelter commemorates the sailing of the *Ark* and the *Dove* in 1663 to colonise Maryland. Westward the promenade narrows, passing seaward of the Royal Yacht Squadron, with its round tower and look-out, the hub of Cowes Week, where crowds gather all day hoping for a glimpse of royal visitors. Parts of the building are the original West Cowe. The row of cannon comes from William IV's yacht *Royal Adelaide*. Further on, the seawall widens on to Prince's Green, which was given to Cowes by George Stephenson, of railway fame. He lived beside it in a Victorian mansion, now the Grantham Hotel. The long grass bank makes a natural grandstand for viewing yacht races or the Solent shipping: there are always cargo and ferry boats to be seen, as well as hovercraft and huge oil tankers going up to Fawley. At the far end stands a small automatic lighthouse marking Egypt Point. Albert Ketelbey, famous for his light music, such as *In a Monastery Garden*, once lived opposite.

Inland, at Beckford Road, Cowes Maritime Museum displays many elegant model ships, shipwright's tools, logbooks, prints and paintings. A lot of the models came from the once-famous firm of John Samuel White that built warships in its Medina yards. There are also yacht designs by Uffa Fox who used to entertain the Duke of Edinburgh in Cowes Week. Bekens, the famous marine photographer, always has a window displaying its striking prints and calendars of yachts in full sail.

In the High Street, there is Cowes Toy and Model Museum, with model ships and a vast range of old Dinky and Corgi cars, together with trains, model soldiers and vintage toys. Nearby, The Isle of Wight Model Railway claims to have one of the largest and most spectacular layouts in the world, where historic trains can be seen running through 'England', 'The Alps' and 'The Prairies'.

Getting the wind up: a crew prepares for a day's sailing in a calm sea off Cowes

Inset: sleek boats and the immaculate Royal Yacht Squadron cannons, Cowes

Fountain Pier is the terminal for hydrofoils to Southampton, a 20-minute trip, and also the passenger pick-up for the car ferry. The pier has a good view of the waterfront with its boatyards, yacht clubs, dinghy parks and jetties. In summer there are pleasure cruises to Portsmouth and round the Solent.

Inland lies Northwood Park, with its ornate gateway. It is open to the public, with lawns, mature trees, putting, bowls, a croquet lawn and tennis courts all surrounding Northwood House. This is a classical-style mansion built in 1837 for the Ward family. Although now partly council offices, it is still the scene of grand balls during Cowes Week, which ends with the great Cowes fireworks over the harbour.

Below stands St Mary's Church, largely rebuilt by the Wards in 1867, to the designs of John Nash.

AA recommends:

Hotels: Holmwood, Egypt Point, 3-star, *tel.* (0983) 292508

Cowes, 260 Arctic Rd, West Cowes, 2-star, *tel.* (0983) 291541

Fountain, High St, 2-star, *tel.* (0983) 292397

Restaurant: G's Restaurant, 10 Bath Rd, 1-fork, *tel.* (0983) 297021

Campsite: Gurnard Pines Holiday Village, 3-pennants, *tel.* (0983) 292395 (1m W Gurnard)

Garage: Osborne (Borough Hall Mtrs), *tel.* (0983) 295261

Fishbourne

Map Ref: 85SZ5592

From across Wootton Creek, Fishbourne's eastern bank appears to be green and wooded above the boatyards at shore level, but these trees hide the hamlet of Fishbourne, known to many motorists only as the terminal of the Portsmouth car ferry. Turn right here for the main road, but turn left and you come to old Fishbourne, the Point, which is a circular green surrounding one huge old tree. Beyond this lie the boathouses, another small green and the Solent shore.

In the 14th century, the Abbot of nearby Quarr built stone fortifications here, from where a watch was kept. Later a Watch House was built. More recently it was kept by coastguards – their cottages are still here together with a private dwelling called The Watch House. On the creek waterfront lies a yacht club and boatyard. A Victorian guidebook notes 'the noblest yachts which have graced the Squadron at Cowes were launched from Fishbourne'.

Boats have plied between here and the mainland ever since the monks' time: once there were fine-weather fares which were doubled in foul weather. From the shore there is a lovely view of the creek

Away from the ferry terminal Fishbourne has quiet sailing waters

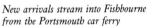

New arrivals stream into Fishbourne from the Portsmouth car ferry

mouth and northern shore. The car ferry looms enormous over the dinghies at anchor, square, blunt-ended and not, perhaps, a thing of beauty, but easy for the motorist with its roll-on, roll-off design and comfortable viewing decks. Just inland from the green a lane turns off eastward to Binstead, leading past the ruins of old Quarr and then on through the grounds of the new abbey.

Fort Victoria Country Park

Map Ref: 86SZ3389

A delightful way to approach the park in summer is by rowing boat-size ferry from Yarmouth Quay, which crosses the harbour to a spit of sandy beach with many waders pottering about its river slope. From here a short stretch of seawall leads along to Fort Victoria, passing small boatyards to reach the massive L-shaped ruins of the fort. (You can drive down to a large car park.) Steps lead up to the roof revealing a whole panorama of the Solent. This is a wonderful grandstand for

watching the start of the Fastnet or Power Boat Races, although it is interesting at any time since all shipping is forced to come in close on this shore by the long arm of the Hurst that juts out from the mainland. The lighthouse and castle seem very close: Charles I was taken there from Carisbrooke on his journey to execution.

One of Fort Victoria's cannons; in 1840 there were about 50 of them

The fort houses a small museum, a café and a marine aquarium with tanks displaying the fish from around the Island's shores, tropical fish and some impressive conger eels. Some of the huge gun ports have been left empty – each will take two cars with a view straight out to sea. All around the outer walls wide grassy areas fringe the beach: tables and a barbecue site make them ideal for picnics. The beach itself (of sand, rock and pebble) is dangerous for bathing because the ships sailing so close inshore send in a tremendous wash. Behind the beach, paths climb up through the woods to meet with the old road that joins this fort to Fort Albert further west. This is a pretty, tree-hung path with occasional seats and gaps through the woods revealing the sea below and the mainland shore.

Freshwater

Map Ref: 86SZ3387

With its long, busy shopping street, car parks and supermarkets, Freshwater has the air of a town. In fact, it has the status of a village and gives its name to a sprawl of built-up roads which originally joined the hamlets of Easton, Weston and Norton, Sutton and Middleton. These names still appear, except for Sutton (South One) which has become Freshwater Bay. The building of all the West Wight forts brought work and more houses, some built by army officers for themselves. After Alfred Tennyson bought Farringford, under the downs, the whole area became much sought after by the artists and intellectuals of the time. Today it is difficult to see where Freshwater ends and Totland or Colwell begin, but the original Freshwater lies by the River Yar. Here a few old cottages cluster round the church, and an embankment takes road across river with a lovely view downstream between green, bird-haunted banks to the distant yacht masts and church tower of Yarmouth.

Horseshoe-shaped Freshwater Bay has a steep pebbly beach and a short promenade rimmed by low cliffs of white chalk. A few hundred yards inland is the source of the River Yar, which flows north through marshland to Yarmouth

All Saints, standing on a hillock, is one of six Island churches mentioned in the Domesday Book. The 19th-century expansion of Freshwater necessitated enlarging the building from one gable to three and it became very much the Tennyson's church. Sir John Stainer composed a special tune for the clock and called it *The Tennyson Chimes*. G F Watts, the painter who had followed them to Freshwater, designed one of the stained glass windows on a Tennyson poem – the angel's face in it is a portrait of Lady Tennyson. Various memorials to members of the family decorate the walls: a statue of St John commemorates Lionel Tennyson who died young, at sea. There are more family memorials in the churchyard from where there is a vast view. In spring the whole churchyard is carpeted with crocuses and many ornamental trees have recently been planted to take the place of elms killed by the Dutch elm disease epidemic. A walk through the fields to Yarmouth begins by the wall. Down by the

causeway, paths turn off through the marshes to Yarmouth and Freshwater, following the line of the old railway.

Part of the shopping street fronts a stream with lawns, trees and seats above it. Between the shops, narrow alleyways lead back to lanes leading in turn to Golden Hill Fort Country Park, a pleasant green hill to ramble round, with Solent views and seats for picnics. The circular fort, entered by a massive tunnel through the walls, is now mainly a craft centre where potters, jewellers or coppersmiths can be watched at work. There is also a pub and a café with outdoor tables in summer. Car entry is from the Colwell road.

AA recommends:
Hotel: Albion, 3-star, *tel.* (0983) 753631
Self Catering: Cameron House, Terrace Ln, Freshwater Bay (flats), *tel.* (0983) 752788
Mountfield Holiday Park, Norton Green (bungalows, chalets, flats and cottage), *tel.* (0983) 752993
Guesthouse: Blenheim House, Gate Ln, *tel.* (0983) 752858

Freshwater Bay

Map Ref: 86SZ3485

Come round a bend from the west, and suddenly waves can be seen thundering in, smashing on dramatic chalk stacks in clouds of spray above road level. The bay is a mere circular nick in the tall, white cliffs walling the sea. The first building on its wild shore, a pub called The Cabin, was frequented by the artist George Morland who had fled here from his London creditors and painted many pictures of this coast. More hotels followed and Freshwater Cave was one of the sights of the Island. Unfortunately, most of the cave was filled in when a fort was built above it. There are many caves with romantic stories, such as Lord Holmes' Parlour, but these can only be reached by boat.

After the Tennysons bought Farringford, visitors both famous and ordinary flocked to the bay. Today the house is a hotel beautifully situated at the end of a long drive among acres of green lawns just inland from the bay. It still has the Tennysons' visitors book full of the celebrities of the time: Edward Lear, Anthony Trollope and Lewis Carroll, for example, and Lord Alfred's study is kept as he furnished it. Another famous resident was Julia Cameron, the pioneer portrait photographer who knocked two cottages into one and called it Dimbola after the family's coffee plantation in Ceylon. She would rush out and seize any passer-by who had a face suitable for modelling.

By this century the bay community was large enough to need a church of its own, so in 1908 St Agnes was built. Long and low like a beautiful barn, it is the only thatched church on the Island.

Top: the 80-year-old thatched church of St Agnes, unique on the Island

Inside, clear glass windows frame the cliff meadows. There is a photograph of 'St Agnes' on the wall – it is Julia Cameron's maid, Margaret. The site was given by the second Lord Tennyson and the porch by his wife.

When the forts were built, so much shingle was taken from the shore that the sea burst through one stormy night, cascading into the head waters of the River Yar, so turning all the land west into the Isle of Freshwater, its ancient name. Today a high, broad seawall cuts off the shore from the river and makes a pleasant stroll round the bay where a few fishing boats anchor and herring gulls cry. There are several hotels and cafés, one of them in the old Redoubt with a spectacular view of the coast. The bay offers splendid cliff walks in either direction (the path to The Needles turns off near Dimbola), and unspoiled downland with the Tennyson Trail along its crest. Just above the bay, the golf course has airy views of the Channel and the Solent. Down in the bay, behind a large car park, there are walks through the marshes to Freshwater town – in summer a nature lover's paradise of wild flowers and

Above: sculptor Peter Evans at work at Golden Hill Fort Craft Centre

butterflies. Earlier, seabirds flock to the stacks in the bay to nest and from the eastern clifftop you can look down on the Mermaid, Arch and Stag Rocks, white with gulls.

Gatcombe

Map Ref: 90SZ4985

Sheltered in a green valley between the downs, the little village of Gatcombe is one of the most peaceful on the Island. It is a cul-de-sac, with a narrow road petering out into farm tracks and fields alive with larks. Once there were quarries here, providing stone for the building of Carisbrooke Castle; each stone, it is said, passed along a human chain to the site two miles away. The church dates in part from the 13th century, with a later tower and a ring of gargoyles. Inside are some lovely stained glass windows, an ancient wooden effigy of a crusader knight, choir stalls carved from oaks grown in Gatcombe Park and much more of interest. According to legend, when the full moon strikes into the porch at a certain angle, a small dog appears and dances in its light.

Godshill

Map Ref: 91SZ5281

A village street lined with old thatched cottages, roses round the doors, flowery gardens, an olde worlde air, this is what thousands of visitors flock to Godshill to see every summer. There is the Old Smithy, antiques and curio shops, cream teas in pretty gardens, a wishing well, the Witch's Brewery, a toy museum and the model village. The Natural History Centre has tropical aquariums, together with a vast collection of sea shells and mineral stones, housed in a 17th-century house. Godshill is pleasant to visit in winter, too, when the crowds are gone and its period buildings can be better appreciated – Stone Cross, for example, dates from 1600.

The history of Godshill is tied up with the Worsley family of Appuldurcombe. This mansion is actually in the next village of Wroxall, but a green walk to it starts opposite the car park, following the old carriage drive up through the woods and under an ornate three-arched entrance to Appuldurcombe Park, called Freemantle Gate.

In the village, the 1896 school house was built by Lord Yarborough, a later owner of Appuldurcombe. The neighbouring cottage has the Worsley's griffin insignia over the front door. The Griffin names a pub, too, with tall, Tudor-style chimneys, but was actually also built by Lord Yarborough. Princess Beatrice used to patronise Essex Cottage tea gardens on her drives round the Island.

The chief glory of Godshill is its church perched high above the village. According to legend its original builders laid the foundations in a more easily accessible flat site, but every morning the stones were found to have been transferred to the hilltop. The builders finally gave in and built the church on its commanding knoll. Round its gate cluster another group of picturesque old cottages. Old Bell Cottage was once a pub. The church itself, a beautiful light building, dates in part from the 14th century. There are full-length effigies of the Leighs, earlier owners of Appuldurcombe, florid memorials to the Worsleys and much else of interest, but its unique feature is the Lily Cross. This is a wall painting, probably 15th century, whitewashed over at the

Déjà vu? Godshill, which exemplifies rural England, can be seen again at the intriguing model village (inset)

time of the Restoration and rediscovered in Victorian times. It depicts Christ crucified on a triple-branching lily, the stamens still golden and clear.

AA recommends:
Garage: Sandford, *tel.* (0983) 840211

Gurnard

Map Ref: 84SZ4795

A gurnet, which gave its name to the village, is a large-headed sea fish still to be seen on Gurnard Sailing Club badge. The centre of the village – church, shops and villas – is largely Victorian or more modern, and mostly of brick. The more interesting parts lie below, by the sea. Gurnard Marsh is covered with beach chalets now, but the Romans had a villa here, sadly eroded by the sea. Long before Cowes became important, Gurnard was a significant landing site, where Charles II landed in 1671. There are beach cafés here, small boats moored in the mouth of a stream called the Luck, and cliff walks to the west.

The eastern beach, which is sandier, has a few beach huts, cafés and a sloping grassy bank behind it, with wide views of Solent yachts and water skiers. Another small stream, called the Jordan, flows down here. Road and promenade stretch round the coast to Egypt Point and Cowes, a pleasant, flat walk, easy for pram or wheelchair and right beside the sea.

The inland road out of Gurnard

Checking equipment on the slipway at Gurnard Sailing Club

passes one of the few old buildings, at the crossroads. The Round House, where the road toll was collected, is a small stone cottage with a conical, red-tiled roof. Northward stretch the original walls, built with Gurnard stone, of the Ward estate. Even when new houses are built, the old wall must be retained; it still stretches right into Cowes.

The Tennyson Circle

So great was the magnetism of Alfred Tennyson's genius and personality, and the popularity of his poetry between 1853 and 1892, that he attracted to Farringford House (now a hotel) in Freshwater some of the most eminent Victorians of his age – Henry Longfellow, Charles Kingsley, the Prince Consort, Garibaldi, Lewis Carroll, Charles Darwin, Sir Arthur Sullivan and Francis Palgrave.

Freshwater was then compared with Athens in the time of Pericles and there was a meeting of great minds. The welcome Tennyson prepared for his guests is typified in this invitation to the Rev F D Maurice, a leading Christian socialist:

. . . Come, to the Isle of Wight;
Where, far from noise and smoke
*   of town,*
I watch the twilight falling brown
All round a careless-order'd
*   garden*
Close to the ridge of a noble
*   down.*

You'll have no scandal while you
*   dine,*
But honest talk and wholesome
*   wine,*
And only hear the magpie gossip
*   Garrulous under a roof of pine.*

The poems that Tennyson wrote at Farringford – *Maud, Enoch Arden* and the *Idylls of the King* – sold in their hundreds of thousands. From being an impecunious poet during the first half of his life, he became one of the richest the country had known, after the publication in 1850 of *In Memoriam AHH*. He subsequently married Emily Sellwood and in the same year was appointed as poet laureate in succession to William Wordsworth.

His regular visitors were Benjamin Jowett, the Oxford scholar, Edward Lear, the poet and artist, William Allingham, the poet, and Sir James Knowles, editor of the *Contemporary Review* and architect of the poet's second home, Aldworth, near Haslemere in Surrey, built in

Lewis Carroll was just one of the many eminent Victorians who often visited Tennyson at Farringford

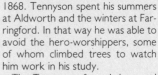

1868. Tennyson spent his summers at Aldworth and the winters at Farringford. In that way he was able to avoid the hero-worshippers, some of whom climbed trees to watch him work in his study.

The Tennysons forged deep and lasting relationships with many Island neighbours, including the Wards of Weston Manor; Sir John Simeon of Swainston Manor; the Thackeray sisters at The Porch, Freshwater Bay; Julia Margaret Cameron, the eccentric pioneer photographer who lived at Dimbola and ruled the lives of everyone who came to Freshwater; G F Watts, the painter: the Hamonds of Afton Manor; and the Croziers of Norton, Yarmouth. These regularly exchanged visits with the Tennysons.

The Tennyson circle was at its zenith from 1865 to 1874 when Emily was suddenly taken seriously ill and could no longer perform her self-appointed duty as the poet's secretary. In 1875 the Camerons left for Ceylon and Freshwater became a relatively quiet retreat, a place to relax.

'So sad, so fresh, the days that are no more'; but for those with a poetic imagination the Tennyson magic still lingers.

Richard Hutchings

Havenstreet

Map Ref: 88SZ5690

On high ground above the head of Wootton Creek, this village has few really old buildings, mostly brick cottages and farms. It was even smaller until the Newport to Ryde railway opened in 1875, giving the village a station. Then John Rylands, a Lancashire cotton magnate, decided to retire here. He built a huge, square Victorian pile with a Grecian-style front and gave it to the village as a community centre; as his Lancashire home was called Longford Hall, this was named the Longford Institute.

Though it dwarfs every other building nearby, the institute is small compared with the house that Rylands built for himself further west: a vast spread of gables, wings and turrets; it became a hospital, but is now closed. He also built cottages and a gasworks by the station – look for his monogram all round this agricultural village.

After the railway line was closed, Havenstreet station was taken over by a private company, The Isle of Wight Steam Railway. A great deal of voluntary work has restored the station, locomotives and rolling stock so that steam trains now run two-mile trips to Wootton, chuffing through the woods at summer weekends. Exhibits include the Calbourne engine in her green Southern Railway livery, the last to go out of service. Mr Ryland's Gas House is now a museum.

Havenstreet has an unusual war memorial. A steep path leads up a grassy knoll to a low stone wall enclosing a courtyard and a stone building, which shelter an altar and inscribed slate tablets. Although the spot is only 200ft (61m) high, it provides a panoramic view from downs in the south to the Solent in the north. There are stretches of woodland closer at hand, however, with both Briddlesford Copse and Firestone Copse offering inviting country walks.

Lake

Map Ref: 88SZ5983

Although it resembles a red-brick suburb of Sandown, Lake does retain some village qualities. There is the Church of the Good Shepherd, for example, built in 1890 but appearing much older, and the row of small shops which are proper village stores run by their owners. A short walk away is a lovely cliff path joining Sandown to Shanklin, with lawns, flower beds, seats and a wonderful view across the bay to the white cliffs of Culver. Paths down the cliff lead to a quieter stretch of beach, since it can be reached only on foot. The new sea defences form a wide seawall all along the cliff base, so creating one more footpath to either resort and the best for studying interesting plants on the cliff itself. British Rail has recently opened a new station at Lake, near the beach and especially convenient for pedestrians.

Just outside the village lies Sandown Airport, suitable for private planes. Here you can hire a motor caravan to explore the Island, make a trial flight in a glider, or take a course of flying lessons or just a short pleasure flight. Many visitors simply enjoy an hour in the café or on the grass watching the comings and goings of the aircraft.

Luccombe and the Landslip

Map Ref: 91SZ5879

At some time in the past, the edge of the southern cliffs sank to form a great ledge beneath an inner cliff, sheltered from the north but facing the sea. Today the Landslip is a picturesque jungle of old trees laced with honeysuckle and clematis, mossy boulders and winding streams, with St Boniface rearing

In the 'hot seat' of the superbly restored engine Calbourne, *seen (below) resplendent in her green Southern Railway livery at privately owned Havenstreet Station*

The church of St Peter and St Paul, opposite, was founded in the 13th century, but has been much altered and restored. The roof of the chancel is lined with timber from the *Cedarine*, a ship wrecked on the beach a few fields away in 1862: there is a print of her in the church, all sails set. A stained glass window shows St Peter and St Paul in jewel colours and a modern window depicts pale flying angels. Opposite the lych gate, with its stone coffin rest, a path leads on to the downs, the lower slopes here covered in old beech, oak and sycamore. This is known as the Bluebell Wood, a lovely sight in spring, with wild cherry overhanging the path which eventually leads to the Long Stone, and a likely place to see red squirrels. A mile further on lies the little hamlet of Hulverstone, once important to Mottistone and Brook for its school and its Thursday market in Whitsun week. Now it has the only pub for the three communities. Smuggled brandy used to be delivered weekly from Brighstone in a wheelbarrow under a load of washing.

Nettlestone

Map Ref: 89SZ6290

The village of mostly recent houses stands round a small triangular green. This has a few seats, and there is a row of houses opposite named after colleges, Winchester, Marlborough and so on. For hundreds of years the village belonged to St Helens, but now has an identity of its own together with several shops and Creeth's engineering works, the last company on the Island to run steam buses. There is a pub called The Wayside Inn and another just out of the village, The Wishing Well, with a restaurant and large car park. Round about are walks through the fields to Whitefield Woods, out to Priory Bay or to join the Coastal Path to St Helens.

above it. Trees along its southern edge are contorted by the sea winds, while ivy and ferns green the woodland floor. A footpath leads all through it from Shanklin Old Village to Bonchurch. Halfway along, the inner cliff disappears and the land is scooped out in a huge green bowl, the coast road looping round its rim with fine views of Sandown Bay. Where the road curves sharply, a path leads up on to St Boniface, a less precipitous climb than that from either Bonchurch or Ventnor.

Deep in the bowl lies the hamlet of Luccombe: a farm and a few cottages, one of them a restaurant. There used to be a hydrangea farm here. In the moist mild climate the shrubs ran wild so that here the whole cliff seems to turn pink in summer. Luccombe Chine hardly deserves the name; it is a flight of steps (208 in all) leading steeply down the cliff face to the shore. Smugglers used to run up the steps in the dark, each with a barrel slung fore and aft. The cliffs are dark and forbidding above level sand and black reefs.

Mottistone

Map Ref: 87SZ4083

This is the quintessential English village: grey stone manor house and church overlooking the green, with a well in the middle and a few cottages round its edge, doves above and cliffs below. Even its one concession to the 20th century, the bus shelter, is built of stone.

The Landslip, where the effects of underlying 'blue slipper' are obvious

Mottistone is mentioned in the Domesday survey and for hundreds of years belonged to the Cheke family. In 1544 Sir John was tutor to Prince Edward, though he was later thrown into the Tower for supporting Lady Jane Grey. In the 18th century, when it was a farm, a landslide piled rubble over the eastern wing, roof high. The front garden between the Manor wings is broken by ancient stone walls (the remains of old barns) draped with rock plants. The gardens of Mottistone Manor are occasionally open to the public at summer weekends.

Mottistone Manor and gardens

Newbridge

Map Ref: 87SZ4187

Cottages line a road climbing steeply uphill, then swooping round hairpin bends through working farmlands. The village was once famous for its plums, with greengages being sold for £2 a ton. And, sure enough, at the top of the hill a sign reads 'The Orchards'. This is, in fact, a holiday centre with caravans and a swimming pool, but so tucked away that it hardly seems part of the village.

Although the limestone quarries, brickworks and railway have all gone, they live on in the various names, such as Quarry Cottage, Brickfields Lane and Station Road. The mill, however, still flourishes. At the foot of the hill the Caul Bourne flows under the 'new bridge', although it was called Newbryge 600 years ago! A lane beside it leads down to Lower Calbourne Mill. Although it is not open to the public, a footpath passes its millpond full of ducks. The mill stopped working in 1968, but in 1973 it began a new life as a bakery, using the traditional bread oven. Now, the 'Miller's Damsel' trademark for bread and biscuits is familiar all over the Island, a 'damsel' being a piece of milling machinery which constantly taps or chatters. The footpath leads across meadows to Shalfleet.

AA recommends:
Campsite: Orchards Holiday Caravan Park, 4-pennants, *tel.* (0983) 78331 (adjacent to B3401)

Newchurch

Map Ref: 91SZ5685

The great house at Newchurch has gone, only the stone gate posts remain: Knighton was pulled down by the owner so that a hated nephew would not inherit, but its history permeates the village. It was owned by the Morvilles, Hugh being one of the murderers of Thomas à Becket in Canterbury Cathedral; his son John built a north transept on to the church to make amends. Later the Dillington family lived at Knighton. Sir Tristram, the one-time MP for Newport, is said to have drowned himself in the lake that is now, prosaically, taken òver by the Water Board. The heart of Newchurch is a short street of cottages, a post office bowered in wisteria and a church with a curious wooden tower and spire. Founded by the Normans and enlarged by monks, it is very old and beautiful. A soaring chancel arch at once draws the eye. Beyond, the de Morville chapel was taken over by the Dillingtons and is full of their memorials. There is a lovely 14th-century rose window, and a

All Saints' Church, Newchurch was founded by the Normans and enlarged by the monks. It has an unusual wooden tower and dominates the East Yar Valley

modern one of St Francis in brilliant jewel colours. The Thatchers of Wacklands also feature in memorial tablets. Outside, the churchyard stands on a high terrace above the Yar valley with a panoramic view and a tall stone sundial, a last relic of Knighton.

The names of both pubs in the area, The Pointer's Arms by the church, and the Fighting Cocks on the main Sandown road, have associations with Squire Thatcher of Wacklands Farm, a great hunting man with his own pack of hounds. Since there were no foxes on the Island, he had cubs brought from the mainland. He also bred fighting cocks, his champion birds being sent to London.

Like adjoining Arreton, the village is surrounded by farms, nurseries and market gardens; it also holds a Garlic Fair in summer. There are walks along the river or to either Borthwood Copse or Queen's Bower, site of a royal hunting lodge. Winford, the nearby hamlet, is largely estates of new houses. Above, on Ashey Down, stands a truncated pyramid erected in 1735 as a seamark.

AA recommends:
Campsite: Southland Camping Park, 3-pennants, *tel.* (0983) 865385 (off A3056)

Newport

Map Ref: 84SZ5089

Newport, the Island's 'capital', is an old market town with narrow streets, wide squares and hidden riverside quays. Monks built one of the earliest houses, The Priory of St Cross. A straight road from Carisbrooke Castle to the Quay became its High Street, with a road, Pyle Street, branching off to a ford or pyle. Richard de Redvers founded the town in 1180 with three squares and a grid of minor streets. Later it was burned down by the French, then suffered the Plague, but it prospered during the Napoleonic wars, when many fine Georgian houses were built and the market flourished.

In St Thomas's Square, once the corn and meat market, stands God's Providence House with a beautiful 18th-century shell porch. Now a restaurant, it stands on the site of an older house where the Plague stopped its terrible run in 1584. Just beyond, the town's archery butts had to be taken over as a graveyard. Today they form Litten Park, a pleasant spread of grass under mature old trees with seats and a rose garden, reached through a massive Tudor arch. St Thomas's,

Top: Newport Town Hall has changed little since early last century

Above: one of Newport's restored warehouses is now Quay Arts Centre

Left: sunset over the River Medina

large and handsome, was built in 1854 on the site of an older church and retains some of its features. There is the beautiful tomb of young Princess Elizabeth, Charles I's daughter, who died at Carisbrooke Castle, and a fine effigy of Edward de Horsey, Governor of the Wight. Close by, the name of the Rose and Crown pub refers to King Charles, too. When he was being escorted through Newport to imprisonment at Carisbrooke, a girl ran out of the crowd and gave him a rose. The old Grammar School is also associated with the King.

St James's Square held the 'beast market' until 1927. Today there is no cattle market, but a stall market flourishes near the park every Tuesday and Friday. At one end of the square stands a monument to Queen Victoria, and facing it is a bronze bust of Lord Louis Mountbatten, Governor of the Island until his murder in Ireland.

Recently restored almshouses date from 1618 and the Castle Inn from 1684. The High Street is dominated by the town hall which was designed by John Nash in 1813, but the clock tower was added later. Beside it, in Watchbell Lane, the nightwatchman used to ring out the hour: 'Three of the clock and all's well!' The bell is still in place, fixed high on the wall.

Many visitors miss the river because it is tucked away at the foot of Quay Street, a wide road lined with elegant merchants' houses. The Quay has a seat or two for watching the swans, boats and barges coming up on a high tide, cranes unloading and small boats taking to the water. One of the old warehouses has been restored as a squash club. Another, a huge building with ornate iron window grilles, is now the Quay Arts Centre housing craft workshops and art galleries open to the public. In summer a buffet provides snacks on the riverside terrace. Further down river, the Medina Theatre plays host to professional touring companies, providing Newport with opera, ballet, drama and jazz. There is also the little Apollo Theatre right in the town, converted from a Methodist chapel. Newport is bustling and busy for six days a week, even in winter, but away from its shopping centre there are many quiet corners well worth exploring.

AA recommends:
Restaurants: Lugley's, 42 Lugley St, 1-fork, *tel.* (0983) 521062
Valentino's, 93 High St, Carisbrooke, 1-fork, *tel.* (0983) 522458 (1m W B3401)
Guesthouse: Shute (inn), Clatterford Shute, Carisbrooke, *tel.* (0983) 523393
Garage: Prices, Pan Ln, *tel.* (0983) 524320

Newtown

Map Ref: 87SZ4290

The town hall, standing alone on a stretch of grass above a narrow lane winding down to the creek, is a single clue to Newtown's past. All around spread green fields, oak woods and a few houses, while the air is loud with the clamour of bird cries from the mud flats along the creek's many arms – yet this village was once the Island's capital, being founded by the Bishop of Winchester in 1218. Its streets were designed on a grid system, Gold Street and High Street running east to west, Broad Street and Church Street north to south, with busy quays on the creek bank. All this was changed by the French raid of 1377 when the town was burned and never fully rebuilt. Nevertheless, until 1832 it sent two Members to Parliament and the town hall was rebuilt in 1699 – it is open to the public in summer.

Today, Newtown, which has no through traffic, is a green and peaceful corner of Wight and fascinating to explore on foot. At the centre of the village a fine old stone house, once the pub, still

Top: Newtown's ancient coat of arms. Below: interior of Old Town Hall

bears the town arms. Gold Street and Silver Street are long narrow fields now, bright with wild flowers in summer, with bees as their loudest traffic. A network of footpaths threads through the old streets, although part of High Street is still a road, with the church and the restored village pump beside it. A church was built here in the 13th century when this was a new town, but the present plain building, with only a bell turret for ornament, dates from 1835.

Beyond it lies the creek, beside it several large square ponds banked by grass dykes topped with footpaths – the remains of the old salt industry. Sea water was let into these shallow pans, left partially to evaporate in the sun, then boiled down until the salt crystallized. A long, narrow jetty leads out to the end of a great seawall which originally enclosed a vast horseshoe of pasture reclaimed from the sea. It was breached in a winter storm in 1954 and the sea swept in, returning the land to mudflats. The wall is constantly being renewed, although it now stretches for only half its original length. Nevertheless, it makes a delightful walk, with the mouth of the main creek ahead, yachts coming and going, and Clamerkin Lake widening eastward and stretching out to wooded banks. It is a paradise for the birdwatcher, too: waders feed on the flats, gulls nest and squabble on Gull Island in summer, flocks of geese wheel overhead in winter with that exciting rush of wings, and always and everywhere there is the bubbling cry of curlew.

East of the village, lovely walks through Town Copse or Walter's Copse lead to the higher reaches of Clamerkin's Creek. The banks are purple with sea lavender in summer, the oak and hazel woods carpeted with primroses and wood anemones in spring.

Newtown once took 50 big ships; now silted up, it is no longer a port

Niton

Map Ref: 90SZ5076

A break in the inner cliff, wide enough for a road to climb up, joins the two halves of the village. Upper Niton lies in a bowl of the downs clustered round a crossroads. It has a church and pub, and thanks to stone, thatch and trees, it retains a village atmosphere in spite of its shops and bank. House names, such as Springhead, reveal that a stream used to run through the village; now it appears only here and there from the culvert. The church is one of six on the Island founded by William FitzOsborn and given to an abbey in Normandy, but it was extensively restored and rebuilt in Victorian times. Outside is the gravestone of Edward Edwards, the pioneer of public libraries, while over the wall can be glimpsed the stone walls of Manor Farm. One of the prettiest cottages, Nutkins, was occupied for many years by Aubrey de Selincourt, author of many children's books and translations from the classics.

Barrack Shute leads down to the lower village, though it is still high above the sea. It was a mere fishing hamlet until the 19th-century development of nearby Ventnor as

Watching Birds

Where else in the British Isles can you find such a variety of habitats in so small an area? Bounded by chalk, sand or clay cliffs and shores of shingle, sand, mud or rock, the Island has fresh- and salt-water marshes, tidal rivers and creeks, mixed farmland, deciduous and coniferous woods and large areas of chalk downland, all supporting an amazing diversity of birds. No less than 277 species have been recorded during the last 50 years.

Perhaps the most rewarding places to see some of these birds are the estuaries at Bembridge, Newtown, Yarmouth and Wootton, the tidal stretch of the River Medina between Newport and Cowes, and the headlands at St Catherine's Point, West High Down, and Culver Cliff.

Well worth a visit at any time of year is the Nature Reserve at Newtown, a Mecca for local bird-watchers where, for a small fee paid to the Warden, you can watch ducks, geese and waders from well-positioned hides. St Catherine's Point, at the southern extremity of the Island, is a good place from which to see the spring passage of divers, ducks, waders and seabirds from west to east along the English Channel, and to watch for incoming migrants.

The best time to visit West High Down and Headon Hill, near Alum Bay, is between mid-August and late October, when departing migrants often gather in considerable numbers to rest and feed before flying south. More rarities have been seen in this area than in any other part of the Island.

Seabirds breed in the chalk cliffs at West High Down and Culver, but the best way to view them is from a boat on a calm day in early summer. Some colonies can be seen from the cliff-tops, but you need a head for heights to do this and you should take great care.

Inland, the Island's large number of well-marked footpaths give easy access to farmland, woodland, downs and the three rivers. Take a walk along the River Yar from Sandown Waterworks to Newchurch in summer to see warblers, or along the River Medina from Shide to Blackwater in winter to see redpolls and siskins, and perhaps water rails and kingfishers.

Top: a cormorant at its nest of driftwood with ever-hungry young

Above: eyeing up the birds at the Newtown Nature reserve

The discerning might try a visit to Parkhurst Forest or Firestone Copse at dusk in early June to see nightjars and long-eared owls, or a dawn outing to the woods near Clamerkin to listen to bird-song, including that of the nightingale.

There is something for everyone on the Island, whether expert or beginner.

Jim Cheverton is leader of the Birds section of the Isle of Wight Natural History and Archaeological Society

---

a health resort and the discovery of the beauties of the Undercliff. It was then that the wealthy took to building summer 'cottages' – ornate mansions requiring many servants. The Buddle Inn, good for pub meals, stands on a terrace looking out to sea with a stream ('buddle') running through its garden and steps opposite leading down to lanes to Castle Cove, once a favourite landing place for smugglers. In their heyday all sorts of ghostly stories

were told of the Undercliff road which begins here, such as phantom horses and skeletons with beating hearts! All were smugglers' tales for keeping the place to themselves.

Westward a lane leads down to St Catherine's Point, a low, green headland of hummocks and hollows, the Island's most southerly point and frequented by bird watchers at spring and autumn migration times. Here stands St Catherine's Lighthouse, white as a

wedding cake and open on some days in summer. The lantern can be seen for 18 miles (29km) – on its first night in action the cows ran riot on the downs above. Its balcony has a wonderful panoramic view of coast and sea.

AA recommends:
Self Catering: Bluebell Cottage, Church St, *tel.* 01-940 0293
Guesthouse: Pine Ridge, Niton Undercliff, *tel.* (0983) 730802

Red Squirrels

The Isle of Wight is very special in southern and central England, not least because it has escaped invasion by destructive grey squirrels and retains a thriving population of native reds, many still living in beautiful and ancient broad-leaved woodlands.

north and in Scotland, they have remained on the south-coast islands of Brownsea, Furzey and Wight, protected from the grey by Poole Harbour in the first two cases and by the Solent in the third.

Red squirrels are woodland creatures, and you will find it quite easy to spot their signs. Their tracks are easily distinguishable in soft mud

Although rare on the mainland, the endearing red squirrel thrives in the Island's broad-leaved woodlands. It can be seen at any time of year

It is not always easy to see red squirrels. They are diurnal mammals, which means that they are active during the day, but are elusive and shy. However, they do not hibernate, so you have a chance to spot them all the year round. If you are prepared to get up early and walk quietly along one of the Island's many woodland footpaths, you may be rewarded with a glimpse of this endearing creature. Especially good broad-leaved woods are Borthwood Copse in the south-east and Walters Copse in the north-west (National Trust), or you might try the conifer plantations at Firestone Copse, and the great Parkhurst Forest (Forestry Commission). Please remember that red squirrels are rare and are protected by the Wildlife and Countryside Act, which means that you should not disturb them.

Red squirrels seem always to have been common on the Isle of Wight. Indeed, in one text of great antiquity, it is mentioned that the Island was so heavily wooded that a red squirrel could swing by the branches from Bembridge to Freshwater without touching the ground. Whereas red squirrels have almost completely disappeared from the rest of England, and are now found commonly only in the

or snow, with two smaller foreprints placed between and slightly behind the larger hindprints. Squirrels sleep in dreys, ball-shaped nests made of woven twigs and leaves and lined with moss and dried grass. Red squirrel dreys are about 12in (30cm) across, and are usually built in the fork of a tree branch or trunk, often over 20ft (6m) above ground. These dreys are more easily found in broad-leaved woods than conifers, where the thick canopy tends to obscure your view. Finally, you could search for the remains of red squirrel meals. Squirrels are predominantly great seed-eaters, although they do eat a variety of other foods such as fungi, bark, buds, shoots and flowers. When a squirrel eats seeds, like those of hazel or pine, it discards the shell or husk leaving tell-tale remains on the woodland floor. Hazel shells are split exactly in two, with a neat nip in the apex of the shell. Acorns, sweet chestnuts and the seeds of field maple and ash are stripped, the tattered remains being scattered under the tree where the squirrel was feeding. Pine and spruce cones are stripped scale by scale.

Jessica Holm is a writer on squirrel behaviour and regularly contributes to wildlife programmes

Northwood

Map Ref: 84SZ4893

From the main roads, Northwood appears to be a red-brick sprawl, ribboning north from Newport to the southern fringes of Cowes and Gurnard. To complete its urban air, Plessey has a large works here and a vast field is occupied by huge radar aerials of various shapes, from dish to comb, some moving slowly in their strange, silent way. There are a few farms tucked between all the 20th-century building, but the real Northwood lies down a lane on the west bank of the Medina.

Fields stretch away on either side, then the lane reaches a tiny old village with a farm, church and a few cottages under its shadow. Once all this land was covered by forest and belonged to Carisbrooke: a chapel was built here to serve those in the wild northern edge of the parish. There was also once a convent belonging to the Brothers and Sisters of St John. Chawton Farm close by is mentioned in 1248. Today old farm buildings lean against the churchyard wall, bowered in old chestnut trees and dark yews. The spire was added to the church in 1864, carved from oak removed from Carisbrooke Church during its restoration. Beyond, fields slope away to the banks of the Medina.

Northwood Church, whose Norman font was found in the churchyard in 1954

Back on the main road, one enormous field is the permanent site of the Isle of Wight agricultural show. Held annually in July, it is a showcase for Island farmers, with a ring busy with vintage steam engines, sheep-dog trials and ricking events, while the tents around demonstrate the extraordinary variety of Island enterprises, from rabbit clubs to light opera.

Parkhurst Forest

Map Ref: 84SZ4790

Once the forest stretched right across Wight. In the Domesday Book it was called 'The Park of the King' where visiting monarchs hunted deer. A special road was made through it for the visit of Charles II, but the locals used it, too, poaching the deer. On the first Saturday in May there was a procession to the forest with minstrels and dancing to gather May blossom and 'cutting green bowes to refresh ye streets and give a commodius and pleasant umbrage to their howses.'

Today the forest is reduced and the deer are gone, but there are still more than a 1,000 green acres just out of Newport. The Forestry Commission provides a car park among trees, with an adjacent picnic area and waymarked paths. In the northern part, conifers are taken over by splendid deciduous woods, oaks planted to take the place of those felled for ship-building in the Napoleonic wars. In the conifer plantations there is a variety of trees: larch and western hemlock,

five varieties of pine, various firs, cypress and cedar, with ornamental trees being planted along the rides to break the monotony so often found in forestry plantations. Jays and magpies, woodpeckers and wood pigeons live among the branches, wood ants build their castles and it is a good place to watch the Island's red squirrels – listen for the scratch-scratch of their claws on bark.

There is a 1¼-mile (2km) Forest Trail waymarked in blue, and a green one of 2½ miles (4km), as well as a Wayfaring Course for the energetic. Of course, it is pleasant just to wander along the network of gravel roads and green paths, but in this case do take a compass – Parkhurst Forest is quite big enough to get lost in.

Porchfield

Map Ref: 84SZ4491

This is a small, quiet village among the flat, green fields and copses of north west Wight, with a shop, a chapel and a pub to serve this largely farming community. Opposite The

Just out of Newport, beautiful Parkhurst Forest provides many sun-splashed walks and quiet picnic areas

Sportsman's Rest, a lane leads to a long, pretty walk through a farmyard and woods down to the shore. Another joins with the Coastal Path to Cowes. West of the village, at the hamlet of Lock's Green, the handsome, manor-like building by the road is actually the old schoolhouse, built in 1867 and now elegantly restored as a private house. Oak woods lead down to Clamerkin's Creek, its name a corruption of Glamorgan. Clamerkin Farm Park, open to visitors in summer, is designed particularly for families with younger children. There are pens of goats, rabbits, calves, piglets and sheep where the animals can be fed and petted, together with various traditional breeds of pig including Tamworth and Gloucester Spot. There is a café and picnic area, and visitors can walk through copses beside the creek, perhaps glimpsing water rat or heron, with a view of the wooded banks opening out towards Newtown. It is delightfully secluded and one of the more peaceful parts of the Island.

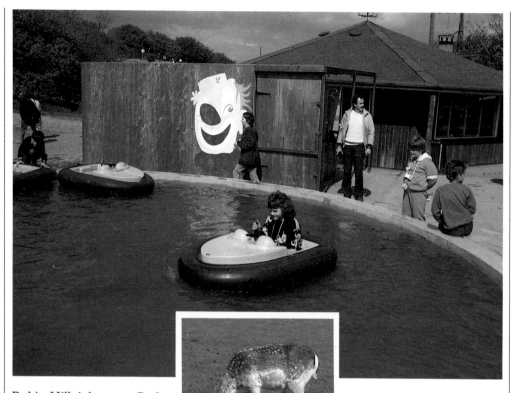

Robin Hill Adventure Park

Map Ref: 85SZ5387

You do not *have* to adventure here, because Robin Hill offers a variety of pleasures spread over 80 acres of south-east-facing downland. At the top cluster all the noisy fun things: safari cars, BMX bikes, Santa Fé railway, assault courses, giant slide, archery, shooting range and toddlers' spider-castle. The latest addition is a nine-hole golf course, teeing off from an island in the lake. All the rest is devoted to animals and trees, a vast green hillside. Aviaries exhibit eagle owls and performing parrots. There is a woodland cage full of enchanting kitten-size squirrel monkeys, a field for ostriches and llamas, a lake with many species of ducks and geese, and a jungle house where turtles, terrapins and snakes snooze among a riot of exotic foliage. But the special pleasure of Robin Hill is strolling around among the free-range animals, grazing fallow deer, little prairie marmots popping up from their burrows, doves and peacocks, and the wallabies in their wood, each mother with a joey peering from her pouch. The woodland has a nature trail for children, and there are delightful water gardens with paths and bridges suitable for a pram or wheelchair winding along streams and pools hung with willows and water plants.

The café and picnic terrace command a view right across to Sandown Bay. There are plans to feature the recently excavated Roman Villa, but at present it is re-covered for preservation. Gallows Hill nearby commemorates the hanging of Micah Morey for the

murder of his grandson in 1776, part of the gibbet being built into the Hare and Hounds next door to Robin Hill, a pub offering a variety of good food.

Rookley

Map Ref: 90SZ5084

At the crossroads in the centre of the village there is a tiny green with a seat, set out for the Queen's Jubilee in 1977. Opposite stands the old schoolhouse, elegantly converted into a private house, and Highwood Lodge, believed to be half-way between the north and south coasts, where carriage horses used to be changed. Otherwise, Rookley gives the impression of a straggle of red brick. Its heart has ceased to beat. That heart was a large brickworks, built in 1924, with a tall chimney dominating the flat landscape. After the war the site lay derelict for many years, now it has become an industrial estate. But the old clay and sand diggings close by have been transformed into Rookley Country Park, two fine lakes fringed with rushes, their banks planted with hundreds of trees sheltering various breeds of ducks and geese. There is also an adventure playground, a putting green and restaurant – a new heart for Rookley, perhaps.

Lake Farm, just outside, has a large stables and riding school, including a large indoor area for

*Above: steady as she goes! Watery fun at Robin Hill Park playground.
Left: fallow deer in the Park*

dressage and pony shows, and where toddlers can learn to ride. Just above it, on the exposed road over Bleak Down, stands the Chequers Inn, an old slate-hung pub used as a depot by smugglers bringing spirits to Newport. To avoid the customs officer living in Rookley, the contraband – often hidden under a layer of fish – was taken by a circuitous route through narrow lanes.

There are walks from Rookley through the fields to Godshill, up through the woods to Chillerton or down into the valley of the infant River Medina, which is bright with purple loosestrife, iris and other water plants in summer.

Ryde

Map Ref: 88SZ5992

Wide and busy Union Street, lined with shops, slopes steeply down to the sea, framing a passing ferry or even the *QE2*. There was once a small farming village on the hilltop, joined to a fishing hamlet on the shore by a lane called Union Street. Since then Ryde has grown into the most sophisticated Island town, the ferry terminal for London. The Royal Victoria arcade is lined with fashion boutiques and antiques shops, with a stall market in the cellars beneath. Behind lies St Thomas's Church, recently saved from ruin to house the British Australian Heritage Society's exhibition; this commemorates the first fleets to sail to Australia from the Mother Bank, off Ryde, in

in with sinister speed. There is a plaque on the front commemorating the sinking of the *Royal George* off Ryde in 1782. Excursion boats from Cowes will land sightseers on Spitbank Fort, a circular mass of granite and iron in mid-Solent, to explore the passages and rooms that honeycomb it.

Inland, on the site of the old airport, stands Westridge Leisure Centre which offers two attractive, heated swimming pools, squash courts, golf, snooker and a spacious, airy restaurant and bar. Next door stands Cothey Bottom Heritage Centre, exhibiting horse-drawn carriages, steam engines and vintage cars.

Ryde (top picture) is just 8 minutes away from Southsea by hovercraft

1787. Outside, there is a pleasant paved area with seats and colourful flower beds.

Until the building of the pier in 1824, ferry passengers landing at low tide had to be brought over nearly a mile of sand and shallows by horse and cart. Today the passenger service can take as little as 8 minutes to Southsea from Ryde by hovercraft. After the building of the pier, Ryde really began to grow, sprouting elegant town houses and terraces. Some emulated the architecture of the new Osborne House nearby, and Gilbert Scott designed All Saints whose spire still dominates the town. Many of the large houses are now hotels. The long front, on land reclaimed from the sea, offers putting, trampolines, cafés, seats on the grass and a view of the hovercraft roaring into land. There are also the vast Canoe Lake and Chinese-looking Eastern Pavilion where dances and concerts are held. The promenade stretches right along to Appley Gardens and continues along the seawall through

Ryde pier spans the sands, with ex-Piccadilly line London Transport Underground trains running right to the end of it. There is good fishing from the deeper, western side of the pier

oak woods and flower beds with a lovely view of the Solent and all its shipping, from yachts to gigantic tankers, and the three Solent forts. This leads to Puckpool Park, another fortification, with a bowling green, tennis courts and café. A fine sandy beach lies below the seawall, stretching far out at low tide, but be warned, the sea comes

AA recommends:
Hotels: Hotel Ryde Castle, Esplanade, 3-star, *tel.* (0983) 63755
Biskra House Beach Hotel, 17 St Thomas's Street, 2-star, *tel.* (0983) 67931
Yelf's, Union St, 2-star, *tel.* (0983) 64062
Self Catering: Solent House, Playstreet Ln (cottage & flats), *tel.* (0983) 64133
Guesthouses: Dorset Hotel, 33 Dover St, *tel.* (0983) 64327
Teneriffe, 36 The Strand, *tel.* (0983) 63841
Aldermoor (farmhouse), Upton Rd, *tel.* (0983) 64743
Garage: Westridge, Elmfield, *tel.* (0983) 62717

Managing the Landscape

Much of the Isle of Wight is still countryside and two-fifths is nationally recognised as an Area of Outstanding National Beauty.

Any one of the panoramic views from its downland will prove that essential management is going on, whether it be in the shape of cultivated fields or market gardens. Let us take a look at the managed landscape. **Downland** Today the number of sheep grazing the downs is smaller and management measures have to be taken. Invading bush, bramble and coarse grass need to be controlled, otherwise they would successfully oust the wild downland flowers.

There are two ways of controlling growth: cutting or traditional grazing. Cutting by hand or machinery is expensive and time-consuming. Grazing, however, is not without problems as stock needs to be fenced to keep it off busy roads, and flocks can suffer from dog worrying. **Hedgerows** Before the advent of the tractor, farm hands in the slack winter months would turn their attention to hedging and ditching.

Laying a hedge involves cutting the stem of the hedgerow tree and laying it on its side so that fresh shoots can grow up. Today, most hedges are cut with machinery, and on arable land even this is an extra expense. **Woodlands** Woodlands on the Island are very much influenced by man's management, whether it be indirect, by allowing stock to graze the wood, or direct, through felling for domestic use or coppicing.

The Forestry Commission manages the larger woods, but small woodlands are equally important, though mostly as an amenity and landscape feature. However, because these woods are not commercially viable, they are not receiving attention. We should not be complacent about this neglect: left on its own, a 40-year-old coppice would shade out any new growth and die. Woodland management aims at producing diversity in tree age and tries to ensure, by replanting, that new trees are available to perpetuate woods. **Rivers and Streams** Two main rivers, the Medina and East Yar, drain from the south across the Isle of Wight, and the West Yar almost isolates West Wight. Other tributaries cut through chalk and these bournes played their part in farming in the past. Some would have served water meadows, to give farm animals an early bite of grass, and others would have provided water for communities and stock, so villages grew up around these watercourses. **Ponds** The farm pond was once a necessity in areas without watercourses. Ponds were needed not only for watering stock, but also to run carts into so that their wooden wheels swelled and stayed firm.

Many ponds have been filled in, particularly in fields where crops are now grown. Others have silted up over the years, showing again how a feature can disappear without active management, in this case, dredging. **Coastline** The Isle of Wight has 65 miles (105km) of coastline, that varies from the wooded estuaries of the north-east to the popular sandy bays of the south. That most of its natural features remain today shows a strong commitment by the Islanders themselves, to their surroundings. The landscape features are a product of active management and in recognition of the need for such management, Medina and South Wight Borough Councils, together with the County Council and the Countryside Commission, have set up a Countryside Management Service. This aims to provide financial help to maintain landscapes, and offers advice and practical help.

Ian Rowat works for the Countryside Management Service in Newport

Below: Tennyson Down towering above Freshwater Bay, as seen from nearby Afton Down

Above left: silage cutting below Headon Warren, near Alum Bay

A craftsman at his fiery furnace at Isle of Wight Glass, St Lawrence

St Helens

Map Ref: 89SZ6288

The 9-acre green at St Helens must be one of the largest in England. With its nine wells and flocks of geese it was the centre of village life and today provides cricket and football pitches, a children's playground and seats, as well as a view right across Bembridge Harbour below. A jumble of houses surrounds the green, from a thatched cottage to a neo-Georgian garage. On one is a plaque to Sophie Dawes, daughter of smuggler Dicky Dawes. When he died she ran away to London and became the mistress of the Duc de Bourbon, returning with him to live in Paris in great luxury – and scandal. Her nephew Edward built the village chapel!

Nearer the sea the Victorians built grand houses with pseudo-Tudor gables or 'Norman' turrets: one is called The Castle. The Duver, a wide stretch of grass and sand dunes with many rare flowers, stretches from the sea all along the north bank of Bembridge Harbour. Walk back to the green by paths winding up through the woods or out along the old mill dam across the harbour. A house here is built with the stones of the old well and stands in its place. On the sea-shore there is a relic of old St Helens, a whitewashed wall – all that remains of the ancient church. Bishop Wilfred sent his priest, Hildila, here in Saxon times to convert the heathen islanders. The Normans built a stone church on his site and added St Helen's Priory. When this was suppressed, the church was allowed to remain, but it had been built too near the sea and the last of its ruins were swept away in 1703. The beach below is sandy and good for shells. In summer a small boat runs a ferry service across the harbour mouth to Bembridge.

The monks' farmhouse later became known as The Priory. Much enlarged over the years, it was a major employer of servants for two centuries and is now a secluded hotel.

A new church was built high up inland, a 10-minute walk from the green along a field path. Some of the tombs from the old church are incorporated within it and many others commemorate families at The Priory. A stained-glass window depicts St Wilfred and St Helena.

AA recommends:
Restaurant: Hay Loft, Upper Green, 1-fork, *tel.* (0983) 872014
Campsite: Nodes Point Holiday Village, 3-pennants, *tel.* (0983) 872401 (entrance off Duver Rd)

St Lawrence

Map Ref: 91SZ5376

The Undercliff road passes through St Lawrence, with old woods on one side terracing down to sea cliffs, and the high inner cliff, a great tawny wall, on the other. For hundreds of years there was only one way down, by the steep narrow shute which begins as Seven Sisters Road. Up here stands the tiny Norman church and a few old cottages – Vestry Cottage was where the minister robed because the church was so small. The 18th century brought the building of country mansions with large grounds. Many of these survive as hotels or flats, their stone walls and mature trees conserving the character of the village. Above the old church, a railway station has come and gone. The mild climate and romantically picturesque scenery drew many writers, including the Russian novelist Turgenev, Jean Ingelow and Alice Meynell. More recently Alfred Noyes, the poet, lived for many years at Lisle Combe – a blue plaque marks the gate. His prose book *The Incompleat Gardener* lovingly describes the grounds sloping down to the shore.

A 17th-century diarist wrote: 'The Undercliff swarms with game, partridge, pheasants, curlew, plovers and gulls.' It was one of the three chases on the Island, still remembered in the name Old Park. William Spindler came here for his health, bought the house called Old Park and drew up plans for a new port and village to the built there. Although he died before this could be completed, chunks of his harbour wall lie about the beach and are known locally as Spindler's Folly. Today Old Park is a hotel with its own tropical bird park. Behind high stone walls a whole series of walks through aviaries enables the visitor to 'rub shoulders' with toucans and macaws, cockatoos and many exotic species, while the lakeside walk reveals flamingos, spoonbills and many ducks. A further attraction is Isle of Wight Glass, a showroom full of beautiful glassware, each piece unique. Here you can watch the glass-blower at work beside his roaring furnace.

Along the main road stands the 'new' Victorian church; its Pre-Raphaelite windows were acquired from the nearby hospital chapel when it was demolished. The unusual west window shows a patient in bed and a doctor checking his pulse.

AA recommends:
Hotel: Rocklands, 2-star, *tel.* (0983) 852964
Self Catering: La Falaise (flats), Undercliff Dr, *tel.* (0983) 853440
Guesthouse: Woody Bank Hotel, Undercliff Dr, *tel.* (0983) 852610
Campsite: The Orchard (venture site), *tel.* (0983) 730381

Up before the beak: a red macaw at the Tropical Bird Park

Sandown

Map Ref: 88SZ5984

A long, safe sandy beach within a beautiful bay makes Sandown a favourite family holiday resort, with the traditional pleasures of deck chairs and beach trays, walks along the pier or trips round the bay. The town grew up round the various forts built against invasion. To the north stand the tall white cliffs of Culver – the ruined fort high on the headland has a wonderful coastal view.

Below it, Granite Fort now houses the Isle of Wight Zoo, which has big cats, a tropical house, a collection of endangered species and an area for children where they can walk among small animals. It also specialises in snakes, offering the opportunity to handle harmless species. Battery Gardens on the cliffs are a pretty park with flowers and seats among the old gun battery walls, looking out over the bay.

An on-shore breeze at Sandown

Other entertainments include the Canoe Lake, a fine golf course, various amusement arcades and the pier with its cafés and theatre, a venue for evening shows featuring many famous acts. The old barracks' site is now Sandown Bay Leisure Centre. It has a large car park and facilities available include heated swimming pools (with a hoist available for disabled swimmers), squash courts, a solarium and a games room, as well as petanque and a 'Trim Trail'.

For the less energetic, *Los Altos* is a vast green parkland with many fine old trees. Ferncliff, above the long promenade, is the garden of an old house that has been turned into a delightful park with an outdoor café among the trees and flower beds; it lies at the start of the cliff-top walk to Shanklin. A visit to the Isle of Wight Geological Museum will open up a whole new world – dinosaurs once wandered Sandown Bay. Today there are bingo, fish and chips, discos and Sandown rock.

Although the hotels are now modern inside, their façades retain Victorian or Edwardian charm, individual in style with balconies, terraces or elaborate wrought ironwork.

Sandown regularly takes a high, often the highest, place in the sunshine league for south-coast resorts.

AA recommends:
Hotels: Broadway Park, Melville St, 3-star, *tel.* (0983) 402007; due to change to 405214
Melville Hall, Melville St, 3-star, *tel.* (0983) 406526
Rose Bank, High St, 1-star, *tel.* (0983) 403854
Guesthouses: Braemar Hotel, 5 Broadway, *tel.* (0983) 403358
Chester Lodge Hotel, Beachfield Rd, *tel.* (0983) 402773
Culver Lodge, Albert Rd, *tel.* (0983) 403819
St Catherine's Hotel, 1 Winchester Park Rd, *tel.* (0983) 402392
Garage: Wight Mtrs, College Cl, *tel.* (0983) 406287

Seaview

Map Ref: 89SZ6291

The village, with its narrow streets and alleyways sloping down to the Solent, manages to retain something of its Edwardian heyday – a leisurely atmosphere and devotion to small boats – in spite of new housing developments around its landward side. 'The cause of Seaview was the Caws,' runs an old local saying. Members of this family bought up a field and built cottages for themselves, handy for their trades of fishing and pilotage, in about 1800, the nucleus of the old village. Picturesque Saltern Cottages once housed workers from the salt pans laid out in the marshes. The long and narrow Rope Walk stands where new rope was once laid out to be stretched. The High Street frames a view of the Solent with the round No-Man's-Land Fort in the middle. The Victorian passion for seaside holidays and villas caused the first expansion: a chain pier was built so that steamers could call direct from the mainland and large houses were secluded behind stone walls. Seaview considered itself select, 'for those who shun the bustle and gaiety of Ryde'. The pier was swept away in a great storm of 1951, but you can still walk along the seawall all the way to Ryde, or eastward into Seagrove Bay where woods come down to the shore. On an ebb tide there is firm walking on

the sands right round to St Helens. A few hotels, restaurants, seats by the sea and a windsurfing school are really its only concessions to visitors. With no through road, Seaview remains a quiet, civilised corner, the only alien sounds drifting over from Flamingo Park.

This bird sanctuary sloping down to the old salterns was inspired by Peter Scott's Slimbridge and opened in 1971. On this wide, green slope, visitors can wander among many kinds of water fowl, macaws, peacocks (mostly hand-tame), sit by the lake among varieties of geese and ducks, visit the flamingos themselves or the tropical house

Anyone for croquet? All sorts of unusual birds and waterfowl can be seen at attractive Flamingo Park

where brilliant exotic species fly among palm trees and rubber plants. All the paths are suitable for wheelchairs, and there are toilets for the disabled.

AA recommends:
Hotel: Seaview, High St, 2-star *tel.* (0983) 712711
Self Catering: Salterns Holiday Bungalows (chalets & bungalows) *tel.* (0983) 712330; due to change to 612330
Guesthouse: Northbank Hotel, Circular Rd, *tel.* (098371) 2227

The Glanville Fritillary

Visitors who walk the south-coast path in late May or June may well be rewarded with a sight of the Isle of Wight's special butterfly, the Glanville fritillary. This insect is found on low, slumping cliffs in a number of places. It no longer occurs on mainland Britain, preferring more southerly climes, but it has for long been known on the Island. The butterfly is quite confiding and you may well be able to approach it closely as it takes nectar from its favourite coastal flowers – sea-pink, kidney vetch and restharrow. If so, you will be able to admire the beautiful chequered pattern of orange and black on the wings. The underside is marked with orange, cream and black. There is no butterfly quite like it to be found along the Island's southern coastline during June.

The Glanville fritillary was named after Lady Glanville, a remarkable lady who, in the late 18th century, shocked the society of her time by collecting insects. She sent her collection to London to be named and it was found to include specimens of this butterfly, which was named in her honour.

The female butterfly lays her eggs in batches on small, young plants of

A unique Island inhabitant

the ribwort plantain, a common enough plant. When they hatch in midsummer, the caterpillars stay together and feed communally, even spinning a web in which to hide. They pass the winter deep in the vegetation close to the ground, and emerge again during the first warm days of spring. In a mild winter this can be as early as February. The caterpillars still keep together, feeding and growing larger, so that by April they are quite conspicuous and easy to find. When they start to leave their webs to find a place to pupate, the vegetation sometimes appears to be covered with the black, hairy caterpillars with chestnut heads. Look out for them at this time of year along the coastal footpaths.

Nobody quite understands why the Glanville fritillary is such a rare butterfly in this country. The caterpillar's food-plant is common everywhere, and observations suggest that it can withstand pretty cold winters. Perhaps the most important requirement is warm spring weather to allow the caterpillars to develop quickly, and for this reason they are usually found in the most sheltered, sunniest spots along the coast.

The Glanville fritillary is very special as the Island's own butterfly and has been chosen by the Isle of Wight Natural History and Archaeological Society for its emblem. Its numbers fluctuate considerably from year to year. One of the reasons for this is that it is confined to a narrow coastal strip which is continually eroding, so that each winter some hibernating caterpillars must be buried or washed down to the beach. But the butterfly depends on these eroding cliffs for its survival and it is remarkable how numbers can build up in good years. Long may the Glanville fritillary continue to grace our coastal undercliffs.

Dr Colin Pope is Conservation Officer for the Isle of Wight Natural History Society

Shalfleet

Map Ref: 87SZ4189

Where the Caul Bourne widens into a creek on the flat northern shore, the little village grew up round a crossroads, church, manor and pub, with a brewhouse and a few old cottages. Up on its mound stands St Michael's with its extraordinary fort-like tower. It was built by the Normans and has walls 5ft (1.5m) thick and no outer entrance. Inside, the church retains simple stone walls and a stone-flagged floor, having escaped Victorian restoration except for some family box pews. Look closely at the War Memorial window, an apparently conventional pair of saints can be seen, but against the sun is silhouetted a submarine and above St George's head zooms a small biplane.

The southern part of the village, mostly new housing, is called Warlands after Walleran Trenchard who once owned the village and was accused of poaching deer from Parkhurst Forest. To the north lies an interesting walk down to the quay. The New Inn specialises in local seafood: behind it lies a National Trust car park – from here one must walk. A lane leads down to the old mill (now a private house), but the main track heads for the creek, a pleasant waterside walk leading out on to a small 17th-century quay built of huge boulders. This used to be busy with boats unloading coal or taking on corn and was serviced by long lines of horse-drawn wagons. Only a stone gable remains of the big warehouse. Now the boats that come and go are yachts and dinghies, and a quiet green corner of these creeklands is the haunt of swan, godwit and curlew.

Boats idly awaiting the tide in the quiet green creeklands of Shalfleet

Shanklin

Map Ref: 88SZ5881

This is Sandown's twin resort and shares the same bay. It grew up after the coming of the railway and the building of the pier in 1891. Although it offers a similar kind of holiday with beach and promenade, pretty parks and a children's fun fair, it has fewer entertainments than Sandown. It is ideal for those who seek a quieter holiday and is a splendid walking centre, with paths climbing St Boniface Down to Ventnor and Wroxall, rambling through the jungly Undercliff or leading to Sandown on smooth tarmac. The cliffs are higher here and also steeper, forcing the shopping centre and promenade apart, but a lift gives quick access to the shore level.

Above all, the new resort has Shanklin Old Village closely linked with it. It consists of a picturesque group of old thatched cottages at the head of the Chine. Once a fishing hamlet, it now caters for

Shanklin beach and the pier before it was badly storm damaged in 1987

Picturesque cottages in Shanklin Old Village close to the spectacular Chine

holidaymakers by offering antiques, crab teas, beach hats, drinks in pretty gardens full of flowering shrubs and mature trees. Westward, across a wide stretch of grass called Great Mead, lies the old church, St Blasius. It was named for the patron saint of wool-combers; and was almost rebuilt in Victorian times, as was the manor house behind it, now a hotel. Jacobites on the Island used to hold secret meetings here and drink to 'the King over the water', Bonnie Prince Charlie. Round about the village are tree-hung sunken lanes, Rylstone Gardens on the cliff, and the Chine.

John Keats stayed at Eglantine Cottage and wished he had a penny for each visitor entering the Chine. Henry Longfellow paid a visit and was moved to write a poem about it, 'Traveller, stay thy weary feet', now displayed at the entrance. Although one must now pay to visit the Chine, it has not been 'overtamed'. It is a great tree-bowered fissure in the cliffs, with a path winding down in a green twilight beside a 40ft (12m) waterfall through ferny banks and mossy boulders to the shore and a pub, the Fisherman's Cottage.

The village is not all thatch and roses round the door, though; at night it comes to life with cabaret, dancing and casinos.

AA recommends:
Hotels: Belmont, Queen's Rd, 2-star, *tel.* (0983) 862864
Fernbank, Highfield Rd, 2-star, *tel.* (0983) 862790
Luccombe Hall, Luccombe Rd, 2-star, *tel.* (0983) 862719
Melbourne Ardenlea, Queen's Rd, 2-star, *tel.* (0983) 862283
Restaurant: Punch's Bistro, Chine Hill, 1-3 Esplanade, 1-fork, *tel.* (0983) 864454
Self Catering: Lower Hyde Leisure Park, Lower Hyde Rd (chalets), *tel.* (0983) 866131
The Priory, Luccombe Rd (flats), *tel.* (0983) 862365
South Wing Maisonettes (flats), *tel.* (0983) 862365

Colourful Shanklin offers its visitors bawd as well as lodging

Here, look at this one! Free entertainment on the promenade

Guesthouses: Apse Manor Country House, Apse Manor Rd, *tel.* (0983) 866651
Luccombe Chine House Country Hotel, *tel.* (0983) 862037
Perran Lodge Private Hotel, 2 Crescent Rd, *tel.* (0983) 862816
Soraba, 2 Paddock Rd, *tel.* (0983) 862367
Campsites: Lower Hyde Leisure Park, Lower Hyde Rd, 5-pennants, *tel.* (0983) 866131
Landguard Holidays, Landguard Manor Rd, 3-pennants, *tel.* (0983) 863100
Ninham Camping & Caravanning Park (off Whitecross Ln), 3-pennants, *tel.* (0983) 862049 & 864243

Shorwell

Map Ref: 90SZ4582

Tucked away under the downs, bowered in trees beneath hanging woods, Shorwell has three manor houses, pretty thatched cottages and an ancient church. It makes no concession to visitors, however, except for the Crown Inn, which provides hot meals and has a pretty streamside garden. Behind it stands many-gabled Northcourt among beautiful gardens that are occasionally open to the public. Beside the road to Brighstone lies Westcourt Manor, an L-shape of mellow stone with a farmyard beside it. A footpath leads past, through Troopers Copse with little bridges across the streams, to Wolverton Manor. This was built by the Island's deputy governor for £800 and is E-shaped in honour of Queen Elizabeth I. This is also a working farm, not open to the public, but the footpath passes right by it. The house is said to be haunted by the ghost of a murdered minstrel whose fiddle can still be heard at night in the long corridors.

St Peter's Church has three aisles divided by arcades of slender pillars. The oldest was a chapel for Northcourt, built in about 1100. The Westcourt chapel was added 100 years later, and in the 15th century another was built, probably for Wolverton. There is a striking memorial statue of Sir John Leigh of Northcourt with his great grandson, and a lovingly restored wall painting, dated about 1440, showing the giant figure of St Christopher carrying a tiny Christ on his shoulder across the river.

Halfway up the steep shute behind the village, a rustic bridge crosses the road. Close by, a small car park gives access to various lovely downland walks. Along the Chale road lies Kingston, a 17th-century manor house, farm, and a little 13th-century church perched on a knoll above the lane which is bright with daffodils in spring. Sadly, services are no longer held here at St James'.

Steephill – Cove and Gardens

Map Ref: 91SZ5576

The tiny bay has a hidden, magic quality because it can only be reached on foot. White cliffs rise up on either side, walling out the world. A few cottages cluster along the seawall, while small boats lean on the sand awaiting high tide and ropes and nets lie about the stones. Narrow paths wind down the wooded clifftop or through Ventnor Park to the resort. A small café right by the shore serves freshly-caught seafood – enjoy it, for there is nothing to do but eat dressed crab and watch the sea foam over the rocks. It is so sheltered here that it is possible to sunbathe on mild winter days.

One of the paths leads up to Steephill Botanic Gardens. The Royal National Hospital for Diseases of the Chest was founded in 1868 here on the clifftop, but beneath the inner cliff. As part of their treatment, the patients worked out of doors in the gardens. Covent Garden sent hundreds of bulbs, the Emperor of Austria planted trees, arbutus and camellias flourished. In the 1960s, no longer useful, the huge hospital was pulled down. Its site is now the car park and the grounds, rescued from years of neglect, became this beautiful park where tall old trees shelter mimosa and palm, orange and banana trees, olive, pomegranate and date. Hilliers of Winchester donated hundreds of shrubs to the park which has many plants native to New Zealand, including the Maori 'postcard' tree. The latest addition to its amenities is a Temperate House, to which botanic gardens worldwide have sent seeds.

There is a pub and restaurant in the heart of the gardens beside a

Steephill Cove is an ideal refuge away from Ventnor's busy esplanade

fountain and formal rose garden. Paths lead up to the wild cliff-edge and a walk westward through spectacular coastal scenery.

The hospital was pulled down only to ground level, its vaults and cellars remain. In this atmospheric setting is the Museum of Smuggling History, where colourful tableaux of life-sized figures show the whole story from 13th-century wool smugglers to contemporary methods, with many local items from the Island's heyday of smuggling on display.

Outside, there is an adventure playground and picnic area – Cove and Gardens can take a whole day to explore.

Thorley

Map Ref: 87SZ3788

A straggle of houses in the flat, north-western coastal lands – through rising land and forestry plantations – cuts out any sea views at Thorley. Its only historical importance was as a rabbit warren providing 500 rabbits a year. Today it lies amid prosperous farmland along the Thorley Brook. Thorley Manor Farm is a fine William and Mary house on its picturesque

corner. Beside it in a field stands a small, curiously shaped building, high and narrow with a footpath leading to it, all that remains of the old church founded in the 13th century. The 19th century brought new roads, bridges and a school. The growing population decided to build a larger church further east, using stone from the old one for the churchyard walls. All that remains of the original building is the porch, used for a time as a mortuary chapel. The 'new' church is curiously lined and patterned with red and yellow brick, while inside stands a massive 13th-century font from the old church. When the low-lying meadows along the brook flood, they are at once taken over by gulls, swans and waders.

Totland

Map Ref: 86SZ3286

This is a village carved out of Freshwater in 1894. Many of its large houses were built by the same architect with a preference for orange-tiled roofs breaking out into small turrets and towers. These were summer residences for prosperous 'overners' – as

Totland Bay seen from Headon Warren, and a local tide guide (inset)

Totland Tides

When full or new
You see the Moon.
The tide's far out
In the afternoon.

But when the Moon's
At either quarter.
At tea the beach
Is under water.

Six hours the water
Ebbs away.
An hour later
Every Day.

Get down to the beach
As soon as you can.
Time & Tide
Wait for no man.

Ventnor, perched on steep terraces, retains a Victorian appearance

mainlanders living on the Island are known. With the Tennysons living close by, the hamlet of fishermen and smugglers grew into a select resort. Today many of the residences are guesthouses among mature trees, served by one street of shops. Above the low cliffs, the Turf Walk is a delightful stretch of grass with seats overlooking the Solent. A narrow road wends down to the beach and small pier. Here, wide seawalls protect the crumbling clay cliffs and provide a pleasant walk around the bay in either direction above the narrow, sandy shore. There is a café and a restaurant, but the bay remains quiet and countrified. When The Needles lighthouse was built in the 1950s, the stone was brought from Portland by boat and landed on Totland beach where it was cut into shape – offcuts of pale Portland stone still lie about the shore.

Christchurch, a splendid example of Victorian Gothic, stands on the hill inland. Its massive lych gate is carved from the timbers of HMS *Thunderer*, which fought at Trafalgar in 1805.

Although Totland merges with Freshwater and Colwell, there are fine walks into open country close by, along the cliffs to Fort Victoria or over Headon Hill to colourful Alum Bay, from where there are dramatic views of the saw-toothed tip of the Island.

AA recommends:
Hotels: Country Garden, Church Hill, 2-star, *tel.* (0983) 754521
Sentry Mead, Madeira Rd, 2-star, *tel.* (0983) 753212

Guesthouses: Hilton House Private Hotel, Granville Rd, *tel.* (0983) 754768
Lismore Private Hotel, 23 The Avenue, *tel.* (0983) 752025
Nodes Country Hotel, Alum Bay Old Rd, *tel.* (0983) 752859
Sandford Lodge Private Hotel, 61 The Avenue, *tel.* (0983) 753470

Ventnor

Map Ref: 91SZ5677

The town terraces so steeply across the slopes of St Boniface Down that the front doors of one street open level with the chimney pots of the next, and all are joined by flights of stone steps or roads zig-zagging round hairpin bends down to the sea. Ventnor is different in character from the other seaside towns. It grew up as a health resort because of its southerly aspect and sheltered position under the downs. Some of that sedate Victorian atmosphere remains, with solid houses of stone and slate, parks and dignified town churches – it used to be called 'England's Positano'.

St Boniface Down, above, provides fine walking country, and it is possible to drive to the summit. Somewhere on the southern face, now forested with evergreen oaks, lies St Boniface Well, which used to be garlanded with flowers every year. Today, the pure waters from the downs are used in the brewing of Ventnor Ales, made locally at Burt's Brewery.

A steep road curves down to the esplanade, past the Cascade and the Winter Garden, the centre of evening entertainment. Little new building obtrudes, although there are all the seaside amenities of cafés,

amusement parks and the pier, originally built to land visitors direct from the mainland. The interesting Longshoreman's Museum presents a display of models and photographs tracing the history of Ventnor, particularly boat-building and fishing, also the local flora. At the far end of the promenade, paths lead up to Ventnor Park on the cliff, with its acres of lawns and flowers and seats overlooking the sweep of the bay.

The first church to be built, St Catherine's, was constructed of local stone in 13th-century style with a pinnacled tower. Later came Holy Trinity, its tall spire a landmark for the whole area. Inside, there is a striking, tall font cover and colourful stained glass. Ventnor's steep streets, old-fashioned charm and beautiful parks simply ask to be explored on foot.

AA recommends:
Hotels: Royal, Belgrave Rd, 3-star, *tel.* (0983) 852186
Bonchurch Manor, Bonchurch, 2-star, *tel.* (0983) 852868
Highfield, Leeson Rd, Bonchurch, 2-star, *tel.* (0983) 852800
Madeira Hall, Trinity Rd, 1-star, *tel.* (0983) 852624
Self Catering: Ashcliffe Holiday Flats, The Pitts, Bonchurch, *tel.* (0202) 622513
Cleeve Court, Bath Rd, *tel.* (0983) 852259
Hills Lea Flats, Bath Rd, *tel.* (0983) 852259
King's Bay Chalets, King's Bay Rd, *tel.* (0983) 853718
Guesthouses: Hillside Private Hotel, Mitchell Ave, *tel.* (0983) 852271
Horseshoe Bay Hotel, Shore Rd, Bonchurch, *tel.* (0983) 852487
Picardie Hotel, Esplanade, *tel.* (0983) 852647
Under Rock Hotel, Shore Rd, Bonchurch, *tel.* (0983) 852714

Wellow

Map Ref: 87SZ3888

Thorley Street, a string of old cottages and modern houses with green gaps between, joins Thorley to the hamlet of Wellow, with its one shop and cluster of old stone farm buildings. Beside the lane leading to ford and footbridge over the Thorley Brook – a pretty corner – stands Brook Cottage, once home of historical novelist Margaret Campbell Barnes. Here she wrote *Mary of Carisbrooke*, an exciting story of Charles I's imprisonment in the castle. When alterations were made, builders found a smugglers' hiding place in the stream bank – Wellow was evidently on the 'export' route for contraband bound for the mainland.

Today it is a peaceful, rural spot with various field walks, the best being the Hamstead Trail which leads south to the downs and cliff at Brook, or north to the wooded creek country round Hamstead and Newtown River.

Morton Manor, one of the Island's vineyards, thrives on the favourable weather, light and soil conditions

The Island's Vineyards

Already well known for its sunny summers, the Island offers other advantages for English wine-growers. Being surrounded by water means that light intensities – important for plant growth – are higher than on much of the mainland, and winter frosts cause no problems. Temperatures below about −20 degrees centigrade can kill vines, but the lowest temperature the Island has managed in 70 years is a mere −9 degrees centigrade – and that was in 1945. With no late spring frosts to damage their flowers, the vines also get off to an early start, one or two weeks before the mainland, and this gives them more time to reach optimum ripeness by the autumn. Vineyards like sheltered sites, and the slightly higher summer humidity could cause a disease problem were it not counteracted by the Island's buoyant sea breezes.

The tremendous range of soil types allows the grower to indulge his whims. Some prefer the heavier, richer soils in the north, and others the free-draining chalky soils in the south. The Island's visitors provide an expanding market for the wines – an important consideration when the cost of transport across the Solent adds significantly to the expense of servicing the trade on the mainland.

There is a continuous history of wine-growing in England since Roman times and yet, curiously, no past record of commercial vineyards on the Island. The honour, therefore, of being the Island's oldest must belong to Cranmore Vineyard, near Yarmouth, which was founded in 1967 and now extends to some 7 acres. As well as wine, a major part of its business has been supplying rooted vine cuttings by mail order. In 1968 Adgestone Vineyard, near Sandown, was started and has now grown to a substantial 26 acres. Its wines have won the 'English Wine of the Year' Trophy, and also the *Sunday Times* Wine Club Gold Medal. Adgestone wines are drunk in places as diverse as Texas, France and Scandinavia. Visitors are able to taste the wines at the winery.

A delightful setting for Barton Manor Vineyard, near East Cowes, is provided by a Domesday (1086) property that was once a monastery. It was bought by Queen Victoria as part of the Osborne House Estate and used by King Edward VII as his Island base. Planted in 1976, this vineyard is being expanded to 15 acres. Its wines have also won the 'English Wine of the Year' Trophy. Although customers include the Royal Yacht and Buckingham Palace, almost all the output goes to visitors to the vineyard, winery and 20-acre gardens. The gardens were expanded by Prince Albert and King Edward VII.

Another very English setting for a vineyard is to be found at Morton Manor, near Brading. Here visitors can look round the house, immaculate gardens, vineyard and winery. The Museum of Winemaking Relics has some highly unusual exhibits. Two other newly established vineyards are at Hampstead, near Yarmouth, and Ashey, near Ryde.

Anthony Goddard is Chairman of the English Vineyards Association

Barton Manor wines have won the 'English Wine of the Year' award

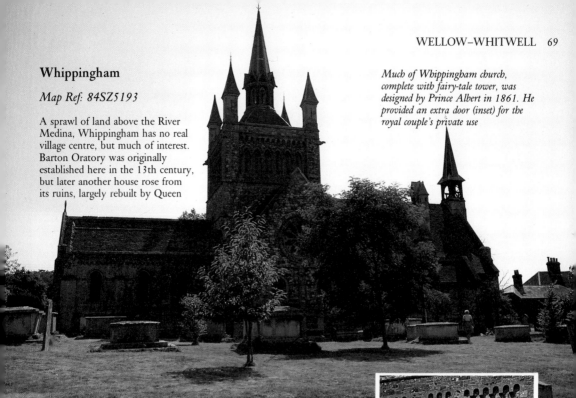

Whippingham

Map Ref: 84SZ5193

A sprawl of land above the River Medina, Whippingham has no real village centre, but much of interest. Barton Oratory was originally established here in the 13th century, but later another house rose from its ruins, largely rebuilt by Queen

Much of Whippingham church, complete with fairy-tale tower, was designed by Prince Albert in 1861. He provided an extra door (inset) for the royal couple's private use

The row of attractive terra cotta-coloured almshouses near Whippingham church

Victoria at nearby Osborne House. Edward VII added wide terraces of lawn. The present owner of Barton Manor has laid out a beautiful water garden and opened the grounds to the public. A few ancient window arches remain of the original priory. Padmore House was a 17th-century farm; now with Queen Anne-style additions, it is a hotel set in 5 acres of grounds with a lovely view right upriver to the downs beyond.

It was the building of Osborne House which really put Whippingham on the map. All round the estate stand houses built for employees, almshouses for retainers and, most startling of all, the church. Here in the placid river meadows stands a tower reminiscent of a castle on the Rhine, with five soaring pinnacles. Inside, there are brilliant rose windows and a large octagonal lantern in the centre, together with royal memorials and a fine sculptured altarpiece of *The Last Supper*. Prince Albert designed most of this unique church. Opposite stands a row of handsome terra cotta-coloured almshouses.

The Folly Inn, right on the river bank, originated in a sloop of that name which ran aground in the 18th century. Today it has a terrace with fine river views as well as a

reputation for good food. Outside, the bank is strewn with small boats, rope and tackle. A walk upstream reveals the river broadening out into a wide lake good for bird watching. If the lock bridge is in position it is possible to walk up to the site of East Medina Mill, where a paddle steamer and a three-masted 'pirate ship' are moored and offer a variety of meals and entertainment. The riverside walk continues right up to Newport Quay.

AA recommends:
Hotel: Padmore House, Beatrice Ave, 2-star Country House Hotel, *tel.* (0983) 293210

Whitwell

Map Ref: 91SZ5277

The village lies along the bottom of a green field in the downs, a mixture of old cottages and new houses, taking its name from the White Well, a place of pilgrimage in medieval times. The well is still there down a track opposite the church, but it is small and wire-gridded. Of the old cottages, there is stone and thatch of 1722, brick of 1867, the old forge and a Victorian postbox. The White Horse claims

to be the oldest pub on the Island, with some 15th-century walls. It suffered a disastrous fire in 1986, but is now reopened and specialises in home cooking. All through the village at intervals stand handsome iron pillars, which are water standards provided in 1887 by William Spindler (see St Lawrence) whose tomb lies in the churchyard. The water issues from the mouth of a kindly looking lion. A lane climbs up the downside, bridging the old railway line, to the hamlet of Nettlecombe from which splendid walks branch off over green summits to Godshill or Ventnor.

A church with the strangest history stands at the top of the street. The northern, and oldest, part was built by the de Esturs and dedicated to their family's patron saint, St Rhadegund. Later, the owners of Stenbury Manor built a self-contained chapel on the south side of it, dedicated to the Virgin Mary. It was not until the 16th century that the dividing wall was removed. Today it is a beautiful little church with its short castellated tower and old churchyard walls. Look inside, and its double history and dedication are plain to see.

Wootton

Map Ref: 85SZ5491

A ribbon of red brick slopes steeply down to the creek and cars rush past, but there is much to see here once off the noisy main road. Downstream the creek is busy, with boatyards on the banks and small craft plying to and fro. Upstream all is quiet with green fields and copses sloping down to the water. Just below the bridge, the Sloop Inn has a terrace looking right down the creek, while just above, Lakeside Leisure Park has a café and picnic tables beside the quieter reach – small boats can be hired for exploring its peaceful waterways. St Edmund's Church retains a Norman nave, a richly carved south doorway, a splendid coat of arms of George III and a long list of distinguished rectors beginning with Edmund de Lisle in 1283.

AA recommends:
Campsite: Lakeside Holiday Park, Lakeside, 2-pennants, *tel.* (0983) 882530

The Fortified Coast

Fort Albert, built in the 1850s, is now a block of luxury flats

For five centuries the Isle of Wight was vital to the defence of Portsmouth, our main naval base. The Island is like a stopper in the neck of the bottle which is the Solent and Southampton Water. It controls both approaches – across wide and choppy Spithead in the east and through the 'back door' of The Needles Channel in the west.

Henry VIII saw that threat clearly and built forts at both ends of the Island in the 1540s. Yarmouth Castle in the west assisted Hurst Castle to defend The Needles Channel that lay between them. Both are open to the public, Hurst via a summer boat from Yarmouth. Henry also built two forts to cover Cowes anchorage 'that in loud thunder roar', according to John Leland in 1545. East Cowes Castle has disappeared, but the fort at West Cowes is now part of the Royal Yacht Squadron's headquarters. Also gone is Henry's fort at Sandown Bay, which defended what was thought to be the best landing place on the Island.

The Victorians were the next major fortifiers of the Wight. Their constant rivalry with France led to an 'arms race' and several invasion scares between 1840 and 1870, before Germany became a greater menace. In the early 1850s, two new brick forts (Fort Victoria near Yarmouth and Fort Albert at Cliff End) were built to support Hurst Castle. Freshwater Redoubt was thrown up to prevent the French landing in the bay. Largely intact, it now houses a tearoom and provides splendid coast views. Fort Albert is now a block of luxury flats, but Fort Victoria, half demolished in the 1960s, still survives amid a modern Country Park; its museum is worth a visit.

A major invasion scare in 1859 led to an expensive programme of modernisation. Hurst Castle was massively rebuilt and 10 new forts constructed on the Island. Four sea-forts of concrete, iron and granite were built on shoals in Spithead to defend the direct approach to Portsmouth. When Germany became the national enemy after 1900, three new batteries were built and many of the old ones rebuilt and rearmed with new weapons. They were manned in both World Wars, but the only ship they ever sank was a British tug in 1915, because she had failed to identify herself!

After the abolition of Coast Defence in 1956, the forts suffered badly from neglect, vandalism and demolition . Today the tide has turned and rescue is under way. Old Needles Battery (National Trust) has two 12-ton Victorian guns and a re-created shell-filling laboratory. Walk down a tunnel from the parade ground and you have spectacular views of The Needles rocks just below. The fortified barracks at Golden Hill, Freshwater, offers good roof-top views of the West Wight and a museum which chronicles the life of the Victorian soldier. In the East Wight, Puckpool Battery near Ryde and Barracks Battery at Sandown are preserved within charming public gardens. And for a truly novel experience, take a boat out to Spitbank sea-fort.

Anthony Cantwell is an author and lecturer, and co-editor of the 'Solent Papers'

Pretty Wootton Creek is busy with boatyards and many small craft

Wroxall

Map Ref: 91SZ5579

While not a pretty village in itself, Wroxall occupies a lovely site in a green fold of the downs, with paths leading over to Shanklin and Ventnor, Whitwell and Godshill. The coming of the railway changed the village, which was once a small agricultural settlement. Obdurate Lord Yarborough of nearby Appuldurcombe would not allow the line to be built across his land, so it had to be tunnelled through St Boniface Down. Many of the cottages in the main street were built for the workmen employed on the 1300yd (1190m) tunnel. Some of the excavated stone was used to build St John's Church, a handsome building with a striking conical tower and blue clock. The railway is closed now and the site of the old station is occupied by a flourishing community centre.

Appuldurcombe, the great house of Wroxall, began as a priory in 1100. It became a convent, then the Elizabethan home of the Leigh

Yafford Mill's great overshot wheel still turns, and all the milling machinery is in working order

Right: the beautifully restored brick and stone mill stands in the small nature reserve and farm park

family and was later owned by the Worsleys, who pulled down the old house and built a Palladian-style mansion with pillared front. Here, Sir Richard brought his new wife whom he married 'for love and £80,000'. Capability Brown landscaped the grounds and a 'ruin' called Cooke's Castle was built on the hill opposite to improve the view! Later it belonged to Lord Yarborough, founder of the Royal Yacht Squadron at Cowes. Since the last war and a near hit from a land mine, Appuldurcombe has been in ruins, but its grounds are still beautiful, mature trees shading the splendidly carved front, with drifts of daffodils in spring. In the lodge a collection of prints and portraits helps the old stones come to life. Cooke's Castle has disappeared, but the Worsley obelisk still stands on the summit of the down above, although it has been partly truncated by lightning. Appuldurcombe is said to be haunted by a ghostly monk who carries a handbell.

AA recommends:
Campsite: Appuldurcombe Gardens Caravan & Camping Park, Appuldurcombe Rd, 4-pennants, *tel.* (0983) 852597

Yafford

Map Ref: 90SZ4481

Yafford is a scatter of picturesque old houses in the quiet farmland among a maze of narrow lanes leading to Shorwell or the coast. The 18th-century mill, built of brick and stone with a fine roof of mellow tiles, is now open to the public as Yafford Mill and Farm Park. The great overshot wheel still turns and all the milling machinery is in working order. Outside, there are old farm wagons and machinery, aviaries, and water, in pools, falls and streams with a spread of flowers along the banks under ash and willow – a lovely setting. The big millpond is home to Sophie and Bosun, a pair of seals who have bred their first pup. Across the road there is a picnic area, children's and adventure playgrounds and rare breeds of sheep and cattle. A nature trail follows first the stream, then an enchanting series of willow-hung pools linked by rustic bridges, home to various ornamental duck, coot and moorhen. Part of the trail is a public footpath; this leads out into a lane beside a trout farm where fish are on sale. There is also trout-fishing in two of the pools.

Yarmouth

Map Ref: 86SZ3589

With its stone quays, old houses and harbour full of boats, Yarmouth is an interesting, picturesque town created a borough in the 12th century. King John stayed here and the Governor of the Island, Sir Robert Holmes, entertained Charles II at his house on the shore; this is now the George Hotel – a plaque marks his bedroom. The harbour has a busy boatyard, the slipway for the Lymington ferry, many yachts coming and going and the lifeboat on station, although it can often be seen out on exercise. A pleasant way to see the harbour is to board the small *Sandhard Ferry* which, for a few pence, runs across to a sandspit on the western side. From the bridge there is a wide view upriver to the tidemill and the downs beyond.

In the square stands the town hall, rebuilt in 1764, various old stone houses and the entrance to the pier. This was once a steamer landing place, but is now a delightful promenade with views up and down the Solent. At the south end of the square stands the church, which was rebuilt in the 17th century; its tower is a landmark for miles. Here Sir Robert Holmes reappears. He captured a French ship in the English Channel and found that it contained a partly finished statue of Louis XIV: this he brought back to Yarmouth where

Yarmouth harbour was originally much bigger than it is today, but it has a thriving boatyard, the slipway for the Lymington ferry and many yachts. Inset: a well-preserved 1930s advertisement

his own head was sculptured on to the French king's body. It stands near the altar.

On the east side of the town, a long stretch of grass slopes down to a seawall. This forms a pleasant walk with seats along the way – Yarmouth offers lovely sunsets over the western Solent.

Yarmouth Castle is so tucked away down a passage by the ferry entrance, that many visitors miss it. As a result of the French sailing up the Solent in 1545, Henry VIII ordered the building of the Castle as a coastal defence. This is no ruin, but a homely castle in excellent repair, where one can wander round the Master Gunner's parlour and kitchen, peer up massive chimneys – even the Great Hall is no bigger than a large sitting room. The open gun platform is a perfect grandstand from which to see all the harbour traffic.

In summer, there are boat trips to view The Needles at close quarters or for fishing expeditions.

AA recommends:
Hotels: Bugle, The Square, 2-star, *tel.* (0983) 760272
George, Quay St, 2-star, *tel.* (0983) 760331
Garage: Mill Road, Mill Rd, *tel.* (0983) 760436

Yaverland

Map Ref: 89SZ6185

The heart of this tiny village is a picturesque knoll, site of Yaverland Manor, with the old stone church close beside it. The Normans built the first house in the village, with a few cottages for retainers, and the church. The present manor with its many gables and high chimneys dates from 1620. The church, though much restored, retains some Norman arches. Victorian rebuilding brought to light a huge earthenware cauldron, thought to have been used by the original builders. This is preserved on a bracket together with several wall tablets revealing that from Henry VIII's reign onward, this was a garrison church for troops stationed in the various coastal forts nearby. Above rises the huge, green headland of Culver, its chalk cave once the home of a Holy Man. He is associated with the ancient town of Woolverton, nearby, which was never rebuilt after being burned down by the French. According to legend, only the stone chapel survived, was put on rollers and transported to Yaverland. Over the church entrance there is a stone head, smiling; it is known locally as 'The Monk'.

During World War II, PLUTO (Pipe Line Under The Ocean), supplying the invasion beaches of Northern France with fuel, passed through the Island. One of the outfalls was at Yaverland.

Directory

The Isle of Wight probably has more attractions than any other English resort. Here is a list of just some of the things to see and do, whether you visit for a day, a short break or a longer holiday.
(Please note that from the mainland, telephone numbers on the Island should be prefixed by STD code 0983, unless otherwise stated.)

ANGLING

Sea fishing on the Isle of Wight is excellent from piers and shores all around the Island. Boats can be chartered. Open sea-angling competitions, both boat and shore, are organised annually by local clubs between May and September.

Light sea fishing can be done from:

Bembridge Spithead Hotel: For Bembridge Harbour.

Fishbourne: For fishing in Wootton Creek.

The Folly Inn: Whippingham. For fishing on the River Medina.

Various fishing trips operate from the Isle of Wight. Contact the Tourist Information Centre at Shanklin for a full list of trips available. *Tel.* 862942.

Trout fishing is available at:

Island Fish Farm: Brighstone. Rod hire and tuition is available. *Tel.* 740941.

Coarse fishing licences can be obtained on application to Southern Water Authority, 58 St Johns Road, Newport, Isle of Wight. *Tel.* 526611.

ARCHAEOLOGY

The Isle of Wight contains a rich diversity of ancient sites that are well worth visiting and exploring. These are some of the most interesting sites.

Brading Roman Villa: Signposted from the centre of Brading. Once the centre of a rich and prosperous farming estate. The beautifully preserved mosaic floors display many unique characteristics. On show in the museum are imported luxury objects of pottery and glass introduced during the period of Roman occupation. Admission charge. *Tel.* 406223. (Open April to September)

Brook Down: There are eight mounds and three different types

of Bronze Age round barrow in the group here. In addition to six bowl barrows (the most common type of round barrow) there is one bell barrow and one disc barrow. Access is from the road between Brook and Shalcombe.

Mottistone Down: Four Bronze Age round barrows (somewhat damaged by early excavators, rabbit burrows and human feet) can be seen. One of the burial mounds in the group, known as 'Harboro barrow' was a medieval beacon site. Access is from the National Trust car park on the route of the Tennyson Trail.

Newport Roman Villa: One mile from the centre of Newport, off A3020 Newport-Shanklin road. Situated in Cypress Road, this contains one of the best-preserved bath ranges in Britain. House built late 2nd century AD. Admission charge. *Tel.* Summer 529720, Winter 529963 (Open Easter to end September)

The Longstone: Stone Age burial mound near Mottistone, with free-standing stone upright and fallen stone beside it. Access is via footpath No 43 immediately west of Mottistone Manor.

CRAFTS

Being such a rural area, the Isle of Wight has a wealth of quality crafts ranging from the Design Council award-winning Isle of Wight Glass to the exquisite Chessell Pottery. Here is a selection of places where craftsmen can be seen at work.

Above: dolls' house maker at Arreton Craft Village. Top: mosaic at Brading of the chicken-headed god, Atarxes

Arreton Country Craft Village: Main Newport–Sandown road — A3056. Watch, talk to and learn direct from potters, woodworkers, jewellers, painters, leathercarvers, metalworkers and others. In fact, find artists and craftsmen of every kind. Admission charge. *Tel.* 528353. (Open all year)

Chessell Pottery: Seven miles from Newport on the main Newport-Freshwater road, at the turning to Brook. Housed in a large, converted stone barn which was part of a 300-year-old farm complex. Every piece is created entirely by hand. Admission charge. *Tel.* 78248 (Open all year)

Golden Hill Fort: One of the fortresses built by Lord Palmerston and now restored. Views from the ramparts, centre for crafts. Admission charge. *Tel.* 753380. (Open all year)

Haseley Manor and Pottery: On A3056, main Newport–Sandown road at Arreton. Try your hand at the wheel in the Island's largest traditional pottery. Admission charge. *Tel.* 865420. (Open all year)

Isle of Wight Glass: On A3055 Ventnor–St Lawrence road. Design Council award-winning Isle of Wight Glass, rich in colour and shape, each piece made entirely by hand. Demonstration from 10am to 4pm during the week. Admission charge. *Tel.* 853526. (Open all year)

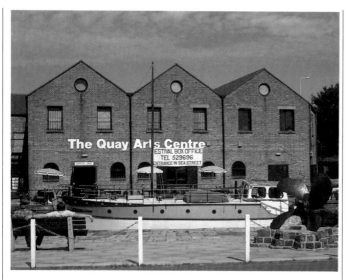

Quay Arts Centre is housed in a restored warehouse beside the River Medina

Quay Arts Centre: On the river at the north end of Newport. Restored 18th-century quayside warehouse. Two art galleries and a dance floor. Pottery workshop and monthly exhibitions such as arts, photography, ceramics, textiles. Admission free. *Tel.* 523464. (Open all year)

PLACES TO VISIT

Castles and Manors

Arreton Manor: Just off A3056 Newport–Sandown road, on the Newport side of Arreton. A fine example of an early 17th-century manor house (Jacobean style) now housing a folk, fabric and wireless museum. Once owned by Cistercian monks and royalty. Now a family home. Admission charge. *Tel.* 528134. (Open April to October)

Carisbrooke Castle: Overlooking the village of Carisbrooke, 2 miles from the centre of Newport, on the Newport–Chillerton road. This is one of the finest moated Norman castle ruins in the south of England. A prison for King Charles I in 1648 prior to his execution. A donkey treads the large wooden wheel in the well-house. Admission charge. *Tel.* 522107. (Open all year)

Morton Manor: Off A3055, main Sandown–Ryde road at Yarbridge Cross traffic lights. Dating back to 1249, rebuilt in 1680 and furnished with period furniture, Morton Manor is set in terraced, landscaped gardens with ornamental duck ponds. Admission charge. *Tel.* 406168. (Open April to October)

Nunwell House: Reflecting five centuries of family history and militaria. Visitors can walk through enchanting and peaceful gardens, view finely furnished rooms and see the room where King Charles I spent his last night of freedom. Admission charge. *Tel.* 407240. (Open May to September)

Yarmouth Castle: In the centre of Yarmouth. Forming part of the coastal defences, Yarmouth Castle came into service in the time of Henry VIII. A Tudor coat of arms is above the Old East Gate. Completed in 1547 and square in plan, it is surrounded by sea on two sides and a moat on the land side. Admission charge. No telephone. (Open April to September)

Museums

Bembridge Maritime Museum: Centre of Bembridge village. Where the maritime history of the Isle of Wight comes alive. Large collection of historic shipbuilders' models. HMS *Swordfish* submarine, salvage and pilotage display. Admission charge. *Tel.* 872223. (Open April to October)

Isle of Wight Museum: Housed in Carisbrooke Castle, its displays include relics of the Island and a small museum of Sir Alfred Lord Tennyson memorabilia. Admission charge. *Tel.* 522107. (Open all year)

Lilliput Museum of Antique Dolls and Toys: High Street, Brading. Home for over 1,000 dolls collected from all over the world up to 1940. The oldest is an Egyptian Ushabti doll from about 2000BC. Each doll has a story and has been personally collected by the museum owner. Winner of the British Tourist Authority 'Come to Britain' Award. Admission charge. *Tel.* 407231. (Open March to November)

The Longshoreman's Museum: Esplanade, Ventnor. Historic Ventnor on view with a unique collection of antique engravings, early photographs, models and artifacts, tracing the history of Ventnor and the Undercliff over a period of 200 years. Admission charge. *Tel.* 853176. (Open May to September)

Military Museum: At Golden Hill Fort, Freshwater. Has panoramic views from the ramparts and is set in one of Lord Palmerston's fortresses. Also houses large craft centre with craftsmen at work. Restaurant facilities. Admission charge. *Tel.* 753380. (Open all year)

Museum of Clocks: At Alum Bay. On B3322, ¼ mile before Alum Bay. Here you can see a unique collection of timekeepers, including superb rare clocks dating from 1590. All clocks work and many chime. Admission charge. *Tel.* 754193. (Open high summer only)

Museum of Isle of Wight Geology: At the Library, Sandown. Dinosaur footprints and a fascinating collection of local fossils are some of the items on display. Admission free. *Tel.* 404344. (Open all year)

Museum of Smuggling History: One mile from centre of Ventnor, on A3055, Ventnor–Niton road. In the Botanic Gardens' car park and situated underground in extensive vaults, the museum shows various smuggling methods used through the centuries. Admission charge. *Tel.* 853677. (Open Easter to September)

Needles Old Battery: Walk up from Needles car park. One of the old Palmerston forts providing superb views of the famous chalk stacks and beyond. Features include an exhibition in the Powder Magazine, two 12-ton gun barrels hauled up from the sea, and a 200ft (60m) tunnel leading to the old searchlight position. Admission charge. *Tel.* 754772. (Open April to end October, Sunday to Thursday and every day in July and August)

Osborn-Smith's Wax Museum: On A3055 in High Street, Brading. Full of mystery and intrigue, and set in an ancient building dated pre-1066. Large collection of lifelike wax replicas. Admission charge. *Tel.* 407286. (Open all year)

Parks and Gardens

Barton Manor: On A3021 Newport–East Cowes road, next to Osborne House. One of England's finest vineyards in a beautiful historic setting. Twenty acres of gardens originally laid out by Queen Victoria and Prince Albert and later extended by King Edward VII. Daffodils, azaleas, roses and herbaceous borders. *Kniphofia* ('red-hot poker') collection. Restaurant facilities and wine tastings. Admission charge. *Tel.* 292835. (Gardens open May to October)

Fort Victoria Country Park: Near Yarmouth. Constructed in 1852-3 as one of the three forts needed to defend the Solent passage. Park includes nature trail through 50 acres of natural woodland. Spectacular views. Picnic and barbecue areas. Admission free. *Tel.* 760860. (Open all year)

Haseley Manor: On A3056, main Newport-Sandown road. A restoration project is underway to restore the ruin that was once the home of Lord Fleming, the judge who tried Guy Fawkes. The property is now decorated and furnished in period style. Also Haseley Pottery. Restaurant and children's facilities. Admission charge. *Tel.* 865420. (Open all year)

Morton Manor: Off A3055, main Sandown–Ryde road at Yarbridge Cross traffic lights. Dating back to 1249, rebuilt in 1680 and furnished with period furniture, Morton Manor is set in terraced landscaped gardens with ornamental duck ponds and parkland. Admission charge. *Tel.* 406168. (Open April to October)

Nunwell House and Gardens: Half a mile from the centre of Brading, off A3055, main Brading–Ryde road. Reflecting five centuries of family history and militaria. Visitors can walk through enchanting and peaceful gardens, view finely furnished rooms and see the room where King Charles I spent his last night of freedom. Admission charge. *Tel.* 407240. (Open May to September)

Ventnor Botanic Garden: Enjoying an almost Mediterranean-style climate, the 22-acre garden contains a rare and exotic collection of trees, shrubs, alpines and perennials, succulents and conifers from most of the temperate zones of the world. Premier garden of its kind in the United Kingdom. Also newly opened Temperate House to grow and collect exotic plants from all over the world. Admission charge to Temperate House. *Tel.* 853526, Restaurant 853254. (Open all year)

Railways

Isle of Wight Steam Railway: Centre of Havenstreet. The railway still runs, and it is hoped will eventually connect with the British Rail service from Ryde to Shanklin. Steam trains run Sunday and bank holidays Easter to end September, Thursdays July to end August. Guided tours for enthusiasts available by prior arrangement. Admission charge. *Tel.* 882204. (Open as above)

Vineyards

Adgestone: Signposted from Brading, near Sandown. Twenty six-acre vineyard and winery. Wine tasting and wine sales. *Tel.* 402503. (Open weekdays and Saturday mornings)

Beautiful Haseley Manor will have no truck with modern high technology

Barton Manor: On A3021 Newport-East Cowes road, next to Osborne House. Six-acre vineyard and peaceful 20-acre garden originally laid out by Prince Albert and extended by Edward VII. Winery and wine bar. *Tel.* 292835. (Open every day May to mid-October, weekends and Easter in April)

Cranmore Vineyard: Situated just off the Newport to Yarmouth road, the vineyard is open to visitors by prior arrangement. Wine tasting and wine sales. *Tel.* 761414.

Morton Manor: Signposted from Brading, near Sandown. Vineyard and winery cover 1½ acres. The Manor was rebuilt in 1680. Intimate and well-kept garden with ponds and parkland. *Tel.* 406168. (Open first Sunday in April to end October daily, except Saturdays)

Mills

Bembridge Windmill: Above Bembridge Airport and Brading Haven. This is the last remaining windmill on the Island, with much of its original wooden machinery still in evidence. Last used in 1913, it is now an excellent piece of industrial archaeology. *Tel.* 873945. (Open April to end September, closed Saturdays in April, May, June and September)

Calbourne Water Mill: On B3401, Newport-Freshwater road, one mile from Calbourne Crossroads. Listed in the pre-Domesday Book of 1086 and operated as a flour mill until 1955. Now preserved in its natural state as an example of a bygone agricultural past. Lovely grounds and tea-rooms. Portable steam engine and vintage fire engine. Admission charge. *Tel.* 78227. (Open Easter to October)

Yafford Mill: Take B3323 Newport-Shorwell road, then B3399 from Shorwell for one mile. A beautifully restored 18th-century

watermill set in the centre of a small nature reserve. Large collection of antique farm machinery and tools. Admission charge. *Tel.* 740610. (Open Easter to September)

SPORTS AND LEISURE

Cycling

The Island is ideally situated for cycling, with a network of bridleways and attractive minor roads and lanes. Varied terrain and steep downs provide tremendous views. Accompanied bicycles are conveyed free of charge on all cross-Solent ferries and hovercraft, subject to space availability.

Cycle Clubs and Routes
Vectis Roads Cycling Club: Honorary Secretary Les Parker. *Tel.* 525396.
Wayfarer Cycle Touring Club: John Palmer. *Tel.* 525707 or 521417 (evenings). Details of various cycle routes are available; these cover distances from 5 miles up to the Round-the-Island route. Also short cycle tracks.

Repairs and Hire
Candyland Cycles: 71 Horsebridge Hill, Parkhurst, Newport. *Tel.* 521120.
Newsham of Lake: 31 Sandown Road, Lake, Sandown. *Tel.* 402783.
Cowes Cycle Centre: Denmark Road, Cowes. *Tel.* 294910.
A Whitehead: Chichester House, School Green Road, Freshwater. *Tel.* 753713.
Vectis Cycles: 68 High Street, Ventnor. *Tel.* 853841.

Golf

All courses are open to visitors on payment of a green fee.

18-Hole Courses
Freshwater Bay Golf Club. *Tel.* 752955.
Shanklin and Sandown Golf Club. *Tel.* 403217.

9-Hole Courses

Cowes Golf Club. *Tel.* 292303.
Newport Golf Club. *Tel.* 525076.
Osborne Golf Club. East Cowes.
Tel. 295421.
Ryde Golf Club. *Tel.* 62088.
Ventnor Golf Club. *Tel.* 853326.

Natural History

**Isle of Wight Natural History and
Archaeological Society:** 66
Carisbrooke Road, Newport, IOW
PO30 1BW. Honorary Secretary
Mrs T Goodley, Ivy Cottage, New
Barn Lane, Shorwell, IOW PO30
3JQ. *Tel.* 740711. Exhibition 'Local
Look' (August to September),
publications and information.

Newtown Local Nature Reserve:
The Warden, Reception Centre,
Newtown, IOW PO30 4PA. *Tel.*
78341. Information and advice on
Nature Reserve.

Sailing

The Island is, of course, renowned
for its sailing, and various regattas
and other events take place
throughout the year. A wide variety
of hire facilities, tuition, fishing trips
and excursions are on offer from
the following companies:

Blakes and Spencer: Beach Office,
The Esplanade, Ventnor. Boats for
hire. Victorian rowing boats a
speciality. *Tel.* 852176.
Cowes Cruiser Racers: 3 Westhill
Road, Cowes. Opportunities for
days out on racing yacht with
qualified skipper, by arrangement.
Tel. 2974941.
Dolphin Sailing School Ltd:
Foreshore Cottage, Woodside,
Wootton Bridge. Sailing on Solent,
daily or weekly. Tuition by day or
week. *Tel.* 882246.
Medina Valley Centre: Dodnor
Lane, Newport. Dinghy sailing
courses. Trial sails on daily basis
arranged. Various types of craft.
'Optimists' for young children. *Tel.*
522195.

Jolie Brise *in full sail off the Island's
famous chalk stacks, The Needles*

Mursell & Kemp (Sandown) Ltd:
Office at Sandown Pier. Excursion
boats to hire for parties. Organised
trips to Portsmouth Harbour and
other locations. *Tel.* 404653.
Odessa Shipyard: Little London,
Newport Harbour. Sailing, rowing
or fishing (tuition if required) in
harbour area. A 27ft launch is
available for fishing or sightseeing
trips. Opportunity to experience
offshore sailing in 35ft (10.6m)
yacht with qualified skipper.
Itineraries to suit individual
requirements. *Tel.* 524337.
Rosanna Sailing School: Wootton
Creek. Non-residential. Suitable for
beginners and near-beginners.
Flexible times. Tuition in 11ft 6in
(3.5m) scows or 16ft (4.9m)
Wayfarers. *Tel.* 882461.
Sleight, Mr J: Woodslades,
Ningwood, Yarmouth. For yacht
and dinghy hire, sailing tuition. *Tel.*
760752.
Wallace Clark Ltd: Yacht Brokers,
70 High Street, Cowes. Can
arrange days out on private yachts
with the owner/skipper. *Tel.*
295712.
West Solent Yacht Agencies: The
Square, Yarmouth. Can arrange
days out on private yachts with
owner/skipper. *Tel.* 760202.
Yarmouth Marine Services: The
Coachhouse, Basketts Lane,
Yarmouth. Generally a commercial
firm, but considers requests to take
a party out to visit places of marine
interest, such as tidal gauge in
Christchurch Bay. *Tel.* 760521.

Windsurfing

A very popular sport on the Island
with a choice of windsurfing
(boardsailing) schools for tuition and
hire of boards and equipment.

Windsurfing School: The Duvver
Tolgate, Seaview. *Tel.* 616257.
Waterlines: 18 St John's Road,
Ryde. *Tel.* 611325.
Wight Water Adventure Sports:
19 Orchardleigh Road, Shanklin.
Tel. 866269.
Yaverland Windsurfing Centre:
Seafront (opposite Zoo), Sandown.
Tel. 404244.

WALKING

Walking allows the visitor to enjoy
the full beauty and peace of the Isle
of Wight. Signposting is excellent
and there are walks of international

Some paths just beg to be taken

acclaim, with the Island hosting
various walking events.

Forest Walks

Brighstone Forest: Mixed
woodland, open downland,
wonderful views of downs and
coast. 2½ miles (4km). Starting
point SZ419846 at car park of
Brighstone to Calbourne road.
Firestone Copse: Off the Kite Hill
to Havenstreet road. Entry at car
park. Picnic place and three forest
walks. Longest walk, 1½ miles
(2.4km), winds through woodland
and along the bank of the upper
reaches of Wootton Creek.
Parkhurst Forest: Old Crown
woods dating back to Norman
times. 2½ miles (4km) with shorter
routes. Enter first at Bulls Gate (off
Forest Road) and drive up to
parking area where the walk starts.

The Coastal Path and Long Distance Trails

The eight trails and the coastal path
amount to a total of 150 miles
(241km). The four leaflets for the
coastal path (see below) and the
leaflet of each trail are sufficiently
detailed and descriptive to assist
those who wish to walk relatively
short sections. All leaflets are
available from County Surveyor,
County Hall, Newport, Isle of
Wight PO30 1UD, or TICs.

Coastal Path

Extremely varied coastline, ranging
from chalk cliffs, sandstone cliffs,
sandy shores to saltings, marshes
and river estuaries. Leave the
coastline at Osborne Bay and a
stretch west of Thorness Bay.
Approximately 65 miles (105km).
Starting point at any part of the
coastline. Four leaflets: SW coast,
SE coast, NE coast, and NW coast.

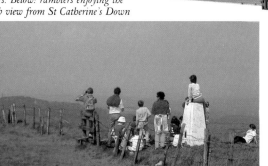

Decisions, decisions! An example of how well the Island is signposted for visitors. Below: ramblers enjoying the superb view from St Catherine's Down

Long distance trails
(National Grid references in brackets)

Bembridge Trail: Shide, Newport (SZ504881) to Bembridge Point (SZ643887). Downland, marsh, some forestry, fine views, medieval villages. Several old manor houses. Historic village of Brading. Roman villa, Bembridge Windmill, varied wildlife. About 8 miles (13km).
Hamstead Trail: Brook Bay (SZ385836) to Hamstead Ledge (SZ405920). Downland, saltings, wildlife, tumuli, Hamstead cliffs. About 8 miles (13km).
Nunwell House: Ryde, St John's station (SZ595919) to Sandown station (SZ593845). Mixed country, downland, water meadows, varied wildlife. About 10 miles (16km).
Shepherds Trail: Whitcombe Cross, Carisbrooke (SZ487874) to Shepherds Chine, Atherfield (SZ448798). High ground, downland, views, plants and birds. Several old manor houses. Villages of historic and scenic importance. About 10 miles (16km).
Stenbury Trail: Blackwater, near Newport (SZ506861) to Week Down, Ventnor (SZ545772). River valley and downland, Worsley monument, Stenbury Down, Appuldurcombe House. Varied wildlife. About 10 miles (16km).
Tennyson Trail: Nodgham Lane, Carisbrooke (SZ482881) to Alum Bay (SZ305856). Downland, marine views, forest. Carisbrooke Castle, tumuli, Freshwater Bay, Tennyson monument, bird sanctuary. About 15 miles (24km).
The Freshwater Way: Yarmouth bridge causeway (SZ347896) to Compton (SZ364855) with spur from Freshwater causeway (SZ349871) to Freshwater Bay (SZ345857). River valley and downland across western tip of Island, joining with Coastal Path at north and south ends. About 3½ miles (5.6km). Spur 3 miles (4.8km).
Worsley Trail: Shanklin Old Village (SZ582809) to Brighstone Forest (SZ432842). Pine Forest, high countryside and downland. Villages of historic and scenic importance. Worsley monument. Appuldurcombe House. About 15 miles (24km).

TRAVEL
You can cross to the Isle of Wight as a foot passenger or you can take your car. There are a number of crossing points and operators. The shortest crossing time is 7 minutes.

Hovertravel: Hovercraft service from Southsea to Ryde. Passenger service only. Quay Road, Ryde, Isle of Wight PO33 2HB. *Tel.* 65241.
Red Funnel: For ferry and hydrofoil services from Southampton to Cowes. 12 Bugle Street, Southampton, Hampshire SO9 4LJ. *Tel.* (0703) 226211.
Sealink: For ferry services from Lymington to Yarmouth, Portsmouth to Fishbourne and high-speed catamaran service from Portsmouth to Ryde. Gunwharf, Portsmouth, Hampshire. *Tel.* (0705) 827744.

For travel to the South Coast for crossing to the Isle of Wight:
Coach Travel: National Express Coaches. *Tel.* 01-730 0202.
Rail Travel: Phone British Rail on 01-928 5100 or your nearest station.

USEFUL ADDRESSES
English Heritage: Richard Underwood or John Paynton, Osborne House, Whippingham, East Cowes, Isle of Wight. *Tel.* 200022.
Isle of Wight properties:
Osborne House.
Carisbrooke Castle.
Appuldurcome House.
Yarmouth Castle.
St Catherine's Oratory, Niton.

Harbour Masters:
Bembridge. *Tel.* 872319.
Cowes. *Tel.* 293952.
Newport. *Tel.* 526611.

Newtown. *Tel.* 78316.
Wootton and Fishbourne. *Tel.* 882325.
Yarmouth. *Tel.* 760300.

National Trust: 35a St James Street, Newport, Isle of Wight PO30 1LB. *Tel.* 526445.
Isle of Wight properties:
Bembridge Windmill.
Needles Old Battery.
Newtown Town Hall.

Isle of Wight Teachers' Centre: Seely House, Upper St James' Street, Newport, IOW PO30 1LL. *Tel.* 524233. Teachers' Guide, publications, information and advice.

The Isle of Wight Tourist Office: For all general enquiries: Isle of Wight Tourist Office, Quay Store, Town Quay, Newport, Isle of Wight PO30 2EF. *Tel.* 524343.

Tourist Information Centres
The Isle of Wight has seven Tourist Information Centres which can assist with information concerning accommodation, travel, events, entertainments and attractions.
Cowes, Red Funnel Office, 8 Fountain Arcade. *Tel.* 291914.
Newport, Town Lane. *Tel.* 525450.
Ryde, Western Gardens. *Tel.* 62905.
Sandown, Esplanade. *Tel.* 403886.
Shanklin, High Street. *Tel.* 862942.
Ventnor, High Street. *Tel.* 853625.
Yarmouth, The Quay. *Tel.* 760015.
(Only Shanklin and Sandown TICs are open all year.)

Any more for the Skylark? One of the boat trips on offer at Totland Bay. Not to be missed

Calendar of Events

Although the items shown in this section usually take place in the months under which they appear, the actual times and dates of many vary from year to year. Also, there are other events such as fetes and country shows which take place regularly over the Island.

Throughout the summer, Morris dancers – the Oyster Girls and Men of Wight – perform at various venues throughout the Island. They are well worth seeing if you have the chance.

In the case of uncertainty telephone the Isle of Wight Tourist Office on (0983) 524343. Full and accurate information about what is going on from week to week is provided in the *Isle of Wight County Press, What's On* – a weekly booklet of events, and monthly Tourist Information event sheets.

April
Isle of Wight Junior Soccer Festival, Easter. Attracting junior teams from all over the country, the festival takes place at different venues all over the Island.

May
Isle of Wight Marathon. Reputed to be one of the toughest marathons, it covers many of the Island's roads through beautiful countryside. Starts at Ryde.

Moreys Festival of Cycling. Takes place in early May over three days of racing and touring, attracting over 1,000 participants. Information from Chris Wasley. Tel. 840399.
Round the Island Yacht Race. With a spectacular start from Cowes, the race can attract over 1,000 yachts of all classes.

June
DEC Schneider Trophy Air Race. Handicap race over the Solent for small planes. Starts at Bembridge Airport, finishes at Ryde near the Pier. Originally for seaplanes.
Round the Island Yacht Race, continued. Visitors still have the chance to see some superb yacht racing of all classes.

Sealink Isle of Wight Festival of the Arts. Aims to attract top selection of the arts including ballet, music, pageants and dance. No fixed time agreed yet. (1987 June/July)
Ventnor Smuggling Pageant. A week of lively, colourful events re-enacting various smuggling escapades.

August
Arreton Pageant. Takes place annually at Arreton Manor reliving, through music and drama, life in Jacobean times.
Cowes Week. The famous international yachting highlight takes place annually off Cowes. Exciting events, the town comes to life and biennially the Admiral's Cup series culminates in the Fastnet Race. Also spectacular firework display from Cowes Esplanade. Always first week in August.
International Power Boat Race. Spectacular start as power boats set off on their race round the Island. Larger boats race further distances. Good viewing from Cowes Esplanade for start.
Isle of Wight Garlic Festival. Proud of their achievement at producing and exporting garlic, the people of the village of Newchurch celebrate with a breathtaking day-long garlic festival.
Isle of Wight Steam Railway Summer Steam Show. For four days over August Bank Holiday.

ISLE OF WIGHT

Atlas

The following pages contain a legend, key map and
atlas of the Isle of Wight, an Island motor tour
and sixteen coast and countryside walks.

Above: The Needles' bright-bleached chalk stacks

Isle of Wight Legend

Camp Site		Nature reserve	
Caravan Site		Other tourist feature	
Information Centre		Preserved railway	
Parking Facilities		Racecourse	
Viewpoint		Wildlife park	
Picnic site		Museum	
Golf course or links		Nature or forest trail	
Castle		Ancient monument	
Cave		Places of interest	
Country park		Telephones: public or motoring organisations	
Garden		PC Public Convenience	
Historic house		▲ Youth Hostel	

◆ ◆ ◆ ◆ Waymarked Path / Long Distance Path / Recreational Path

GRID REFERENCE SYSTEM

The map references used in this book are based on the Ordnance Survey National Grid, correct to within 1000 metres. They comprise two letters and four figures, and are preceded by the atlas page number.

Thus the reference for Newport appears 84 SZ 5089

84 is the atlas page number

SZ identifies the major (100km) grid square concerned (see diag)

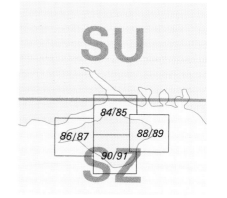

5089 locates the lower left-hand corner of the kilometre grid square in which Newport appears

50 can be found along the bottom edge of the page, reading W to E

89 can be found along the right hand side of the page, reading S to N

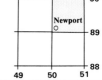

ORIENTATION

True North
At the centre of the area is 0°32'W of Grid North.

Magnetic North
At the centre of the area is about 5½°W of Grid North in 1987 decreasing by about ½° in three years.

Diagrammatic Only

ATLAS 1:50,000 or 1¼" to 1 MILE

ROADS & PATHS   Not necessarily rights of way

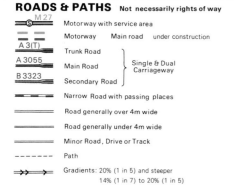

Motorway with service area	
Motorway Main road under construction	
Trunk Road	
Main Road	Single & Dual Carriageway
Secondary Road	
Narrow Road with passing places	
Road generally over 4m wide	
Road generally under 4m wide	
Minor Road, Drive or Track	
Path	
Gradients: 20% (1 in 5) and steeper	
14% (1 in 7) to 20% (1 in 5)	

GENERAL FEATURES

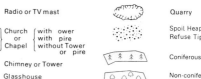
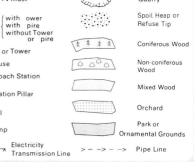

Radio or TV mast		Quarry	
Church or Chapel { with tower / with spire / without Tower or spire		Spoil Heap or Refuse Tip	
Chimney or Tower		Coniferous Wood	
Glasshouse		Non-coniferous Wood	
Bus or Coach Station		Mixed Wood	
Triangulation Pillar		Orchard	
Windmill		Park or Ornamental Grounds	
Windpump			
Electricity Transmission Line		Pipe Line	

RAILWAYS

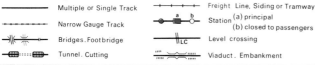

Multiple or Single Track	Freight Line, Siding or Tramway
Narrow Gauge Track	Station (a) principal / (b) closed to passengers
Bridges. Footbridge	Level crossing
Tunnel. Cutting	Viaduct. Embankment

ABBREVIATIONS

P	Post Office
PH	Public House
MP	Milepost
MS	Milestone
CG	Coastguard
CH	Clubhouse
TH	Town Hall, Guildhall or equivalent
PC	Public Convenience (in rural areas)

WATER FEATURES

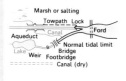

Marsh or salting
Towpath Lock
Aqueduct   Canal   Ford
Lake   Weir   Normal tidal limit Bridge
Footbridge
Canal (dry)

BOUNDARIES

National		County
National Park		District
National Trust	NT always open	
	NT opening restricted	
Forestry Commission	Pedestrians only - observe local signs	

ANTIQUITIES

VILLA Roman	Castle Non-Roman	
Battlefield (with date)		
☆ Tumulus		
+ Site of Antiquity		

PUBLIC RIGHTS OF WAY

Footpath	Road used as a Public Path
Bridleway	By-way open to all traffic

Public rights of way indicated by these symbols have been derived from Definitive Maps as amended by later enactments or instruments held by Ordnance Survey on 1st December 1985 and are shown subject to the limitations imposed by the scale of mapping.

Later information may be obtained from the appropriate County Council.

The representation in this atlas of any other road track or path is no evidence of the existence of a right of way.

Danger Area   MOD Ranges in the area. Danger! Observe warning notices

HEIGHTS & ROCK FEATURES

outcrop
cliff
scree

Contours are at 10 metres vertical interval

•144   Heights are to the nearest metre above mean sea level

Heights shown close to a triangulation pillar refer to the station height at ground level and not necessarily to the summit.

KEY 1:175,000 or 2¾ MILES to 1"
TOUR 1:250,000 or 4 MILES to 1"

ROADS Not necessarily rights of way

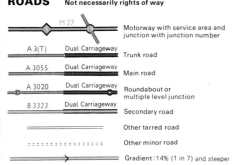

Motorway with service area and junction with junction number

A 3(T) Dual Carriageway — Trunk road

A 3055 Dual Carriageway — Main road

A 3020 Dual Carriageway — Roundabout or multiple level junction

B 3323 Dual Carriageway — Secondary road

Other tarred road

Other minor road

Gradient : 14% (1 in 7) and steeper

RAILWAYS

Road crossing under or over standard gauge track

Level crossing

Station

Narrow gauge track

WATER FEATURES

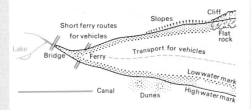

ANTIQUITIES

Native fortress

Roman road (course of)

Castle • Other antiquities

CANOVIVM • Roman antiquity

GENERAL FEATURES

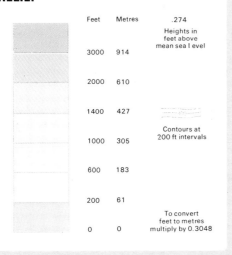

Buildings

Wood

  Telephone : public or motoring organisations

Civil aerodrome (with custom facilities)

Radio or TV mast

Lighthouse

RELIEF

Feet	Metres	
		.274
		Heights in feet above mean sea level
3000	914	
2000	610	
1400	427	
		Contours at 200 ft intervals
1000	305	
600	183	
200	61	
		To convert feet to metres
0	0	multiply by 0.3048

WALKS 1:25,000 or 2½" to 1 MILE

ROADS AND PATHS Not necessarily rights of way

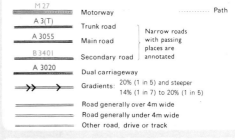

M 27 — Motorway

A 3(T) — Trunk road

A 3055 — Main road

B 3401 — Secondary road

Narrow roads with passing places are annotated

A 3020 — Dual carriageway

Gradients: 20% (1 in 5) and steeper
14% (1 in 7) to 20% (1 in 5)

Road generally over 4m wide

Road generally under 4m wide

Other road, drive or track

.... Path

RAILWAYS

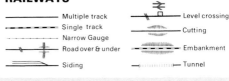

Multiple track

Single track

Narrow Gauge

Road over & under

Siding

Level crossing

Cutting

Embankment

Tunnel

GENERAL FEATURES

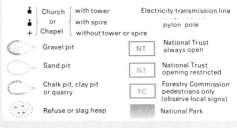

Church or Chapel { with tower / with spire / without tower or spire

Gravel pit

Sand pit

Chalk pit, clay pit or quarry

Refuse or slag heap

Electricity transmission line
pylon pole

NT National Trust always open

NT National Trust opening restricted

FC Forestry Commission pedestrians only (observe local signs)

National Park

HEIGHTS AND ROCK FEATURES

Contours are at 5 metres vertical interval

50 · } Determined by { ground survey
285 · } air survey

Surface heights are to the nearest metre above mean sea level.
Heights shown close to a triangulation pillar refer to the station height at ground level and not necessarily to the summit.

Vertical Face

Loose rock Boulders Outcrop Scree

PUBLIC RIGHTS OF WAY

Public rights of way shown in this guide may not be evident on the ground

} Public Paths { Footpath / Bridleway

+ + + + + By-way open to all traffic

Road used as a public path

Public rights of way indicated by these symbols have been derived from Definitive Maps as amended by later enactments or instruments held by Ordnance Survey on 1st October 1984 and are shown subject to the limitations imposed by the scale of mapping

Later information may be obtained from the appropriate County Council.

The representation on this map of any other road, track or path is no evidence of the existence of a right of way.

WALKS AND TOURS (All Scales)

7 Start point of walk

Route of walk

Line of walk

Alternative route

1 Start point of tour

Route of tour

Featured tour

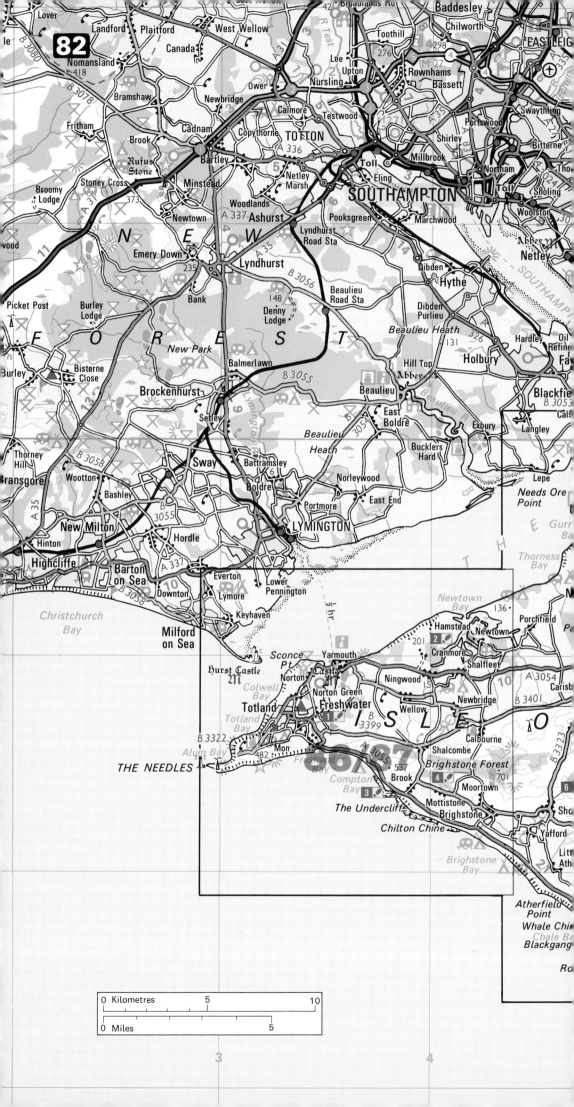

Key to Atlas pages

Distances in miles to NEWPORT
Map Ref: 84 SZ 5089

Birmingham	153 *	Leeds	259 *
Brighton	55 *	Liverpool	263 *
Bristol	90 **	London	80 *
Cardiff	138 **	Nottingham	195 *
Exeter	112 **	Oxford	89 *

* Via Portsmouth Ferry   ** Via Lymington Ferry

ISLE OF WIGHT

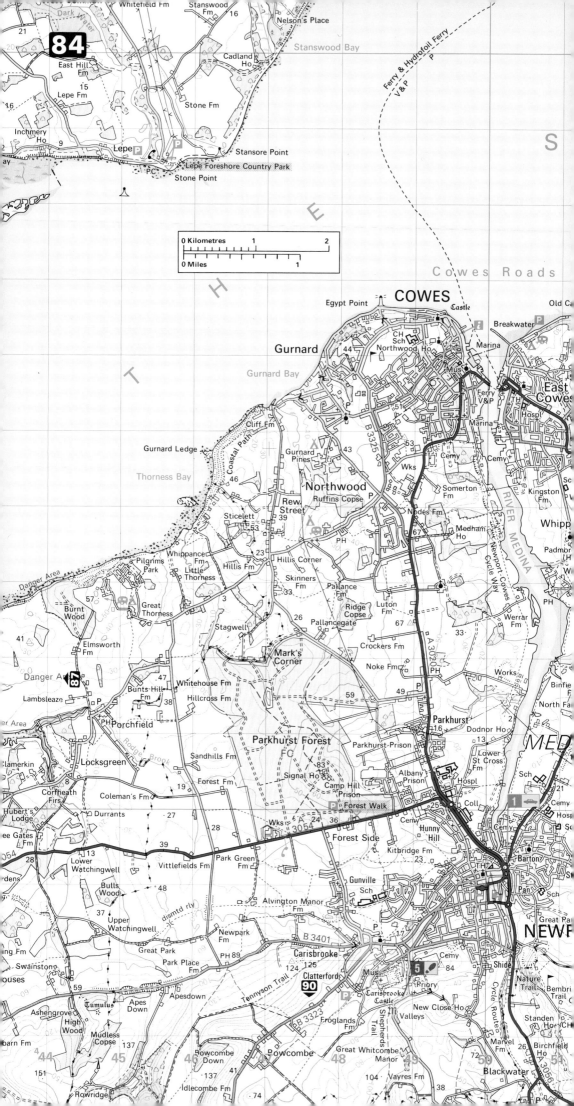

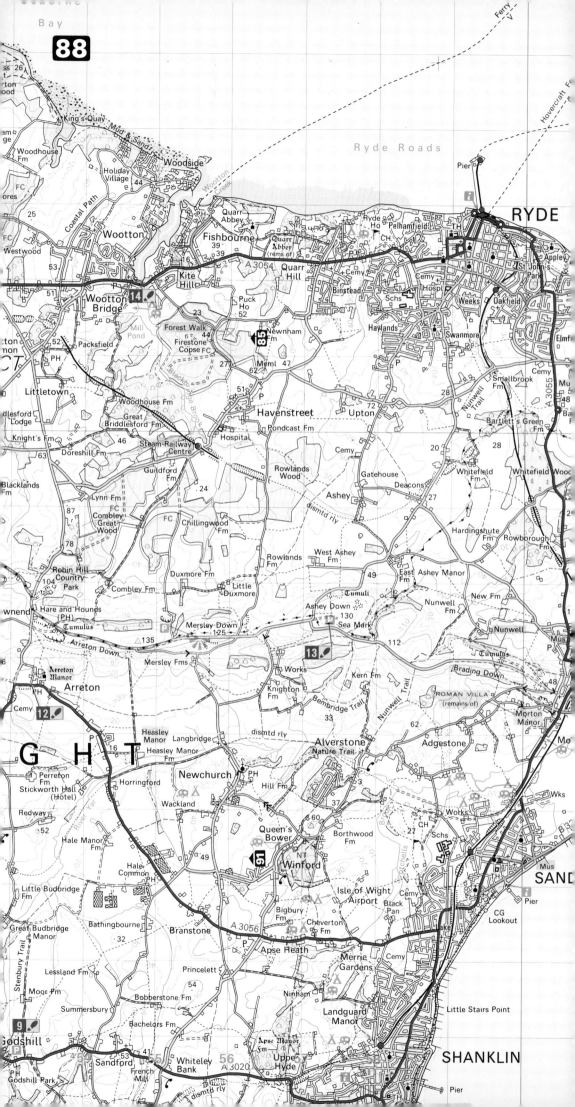

Ferry
P

Horse Sand Fort
HAMPSHIRE ·
PORTSMOUTH DISTRICT

94

No Man's Land Fort
ISLE OF WIGHT
MEDINA DISTRICT

93

s

ool Point

92

Spring
Vale
Toll
Nettlestone Point
oodlands
ale

Seaview

91

Seagrove Bay

Bullen Ho
Nettlestone
P
35
Horestone Point
NT

Park Fm
The Priory
Priory
Bay

Node's Point

90

Cemy

St Helen's Fort
ISLE OF WIGHT
MEDINA DISTRICT

49

St Helens
PH
St Helen's Church
(remains of)
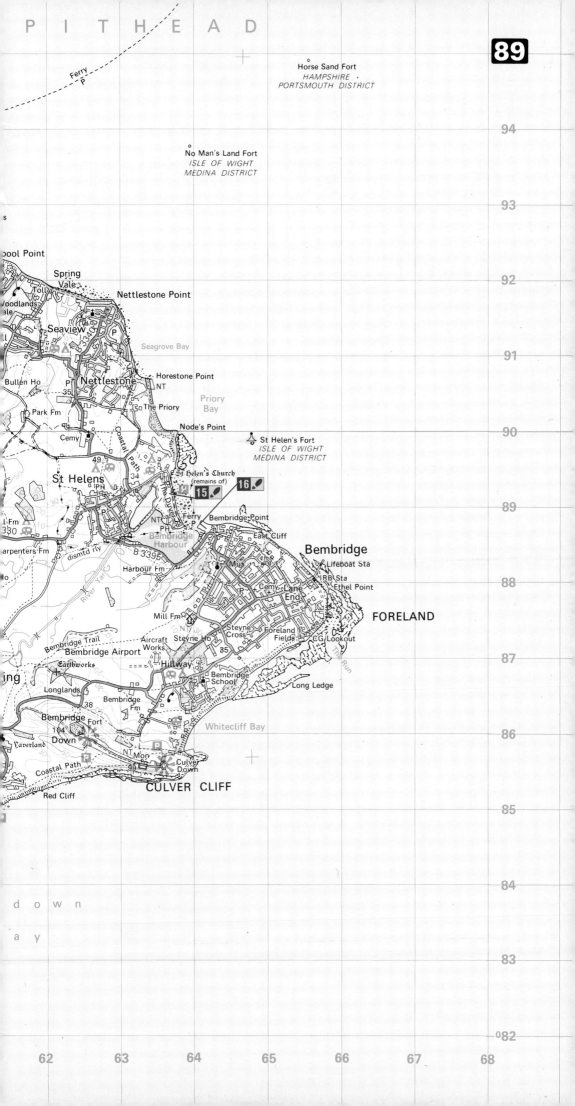
15 **16**

89

Ferry
P
Bembridge Point
L Fm
330
NT
PH
East Cliff

arpenters Fm
dismtd rly
Bembridge
Harbour
B 3395
Mus
Bembridge
Lifeboat Sta
IRB Sta
Ethel Point

88

Harbour Fm

River Yar

Mill Fm
Cemy
Lane
End
FORELAND

Steyne
Cross
Foreland
Fields
CG Lookout

87

Bembridge Trail
Bembridge Airport
Aircraft
Works
Steyne Ho
35
Hillway

Earthworks

ing

Longlands
Bembridge
School
Long Ledge

38
Bembridge
Fm

86

Bembridge Fort
104
Down
averland

Whitecliff Bay

Coastal Path
NT Mon
Culver
Down

85

CULVER CLIFF
Red Cliff

84

d o w n

a y

83

82

62   63   64   65   66   67   68

TOUR 72 MILES

A Round Trip of the Island

The drive starts at Newport (see page 52), the Island's 'capital' – but it is not difficult to join the tour at any location en route.

From Newport follow signs to Cowes to leave by the A3020. In ¾ mile (1.2km) at the roundabout go forward. To the left of the road are the Albany, Parkhurst and Camp Hill prisons.

Two miles (3.2km) further, at Northwood (see page 56), branch left on to the B3325 then in ½ mile (800m) bear right. After another ¾ mile (1.2km) there is a mini-roundabout. A detour to the right may be taken to visit the town centre of Cowes (see page 43). Situated at the mouth of the River Medina, it is best-known as Britain's yachting capital. Of interest is the Maritime Museum at the Public Library, and the outstanding model railway exhibition in the High Street.

The main tour turns left on to an unclassified road (no sign). In ¼ mile (400m) go over the crossroads and descend Church Road, then shortly turn right into Lower Church Road. At the next T-junction turn left (signed Yarmouth) and pass Gurnard Bay (see page 48). In 1¼ miles (2km), turn right at the T-junction, then bear right. In another 1½ miles (2.4km) bear right again and proceed to Porchfield (see page 57). Continue through wooded countryside and after ½ mile (800m) bear right. In just over another ½ mile (800m) turn right, signed Newton. One mile (1.6km) further is the 18th-century Old Town Hall (NT) – one of the few remaining buildings of the ancient borough of Newtown (see page 54).

Continue past an inlet of the Newtown River and at the T-junction turn right, signed Yarmouth. In ¼ mile (1.2km) at the next T-junction turn right again on to the A3054 and enter Shalfleet (see page 62). Later there are good coastal views before reaching Yarmouth (see page 72) – a busy ferry terminal and popular boating centre. The Tudor Castle (AM) is open to the public.

Follow signs to Freshwater and cross the Yar Bridge. Half a mile (800m) further a turning on the right leads to the Fort Victoria Country Park.

St Agnes Church at Freshwater: this was the Tennysons' church, and there are family memorials inside

Remain on the A3054 and in almost ½ mile (800m) bear right, signed Totland. After another ½ mile (800m), on the left, is the road to Golden Hill Fort. A large craft centre and a military museum are housed here.

Continue through Colwell Bay (see page 43) and shortly go forward to the Alum Bay road, B3322 (not shown), to enter the small resort of Totland (see page 66). At a roundabout keep forward and proceed to Alum Bay (see page 34). Here is The Needles Pleasure Park where facilities include a chair lift to view the fascinating multicoloured sand cliffs and the famous detached chalk stacks – and their lighthouse. Also of interst is The Needles Old Battery, a former Palmerstonian fort built in 1862.

From the Royal Needles Hotel return along the same road. In nearly ½ mile (800m) pass the Museum of Clocks then branch right, unclassified (signed Freshwater Bay) with 6ft (1.8m) width restriction. In another ½ mile (800m), at the High Down Inn, bear right then turn left. To the right is Tennyson Down (NT), so called because the poet frequently walked the cliff-top path, one of the most attractive on the Island. Tennyson's former home, Farringford House (now a hotel), is here.

THE NEEDLES

It stands to the right of the road before the drive enters the small resort of Freshwater Bay (see page 46). Bear right to join the A3055 (no sign) and climb to skirt Compton Bay. Here there is an excellent sandy beach. This beautiful cliff-top road offers fine views out to sea with the rolling slopes of Compton Down to the left.

The drive passes the car parks for Compton, Hanover and Brook Chines before skirting Brook Bay and the village of Brook (see page 40). Continue along the coast road for 7 miles (11.2km) (signed Ventnor) to reach Chale (see page 42). Half a mile (800m) beyond the village, at the roundabout, take the second exit for Blackgang (see page 37). Blackgang Chine, a spectacular cleft in the cliff face, was once used by smugglers – the 'Black Gang' from whom it is thought to have acquired its name. A Fantasy Theme Park has been established here with numerous family amusements; adjacent is the Blackgang Sawmill and St Catherine's Quay which includes a maritime exhibition.

Return to the roundabout and turn right with the A3055 (signed Ventnor) then pass beneath St Catherine's Hill, 773ft (236m). The hill is surmounted by a medieval lighthouse-oratory, known locally as the 'Pepper Pot'. The car park to the right of the road offers some fine views.

At Niton (see page 54) keep left (one-way) then turn right. Half a mile (800m) further a turning to the right leads to St Catherine's lighthouse, situated 136ft (41.5m) above the sea.

Continue along the picturesque, thickly wooded Undercliff, with steep cliffs rising to the left, and pass through St Lawrence (see page 61). In Old Park, near by, there is a tropical bird park.

Continue for one mile (1.6km). Here you pass the entrance to the Ventnor Botanic Gardens, with its museum of the History of Smuggling.

Proceed into the town centre of Ventnor (see page 67). This popular resort is given a somewhat Continental appearance by the terraces on which it is built. They zig-zag down to the sea on the slopes of the St Boniface Down (NT). At 785ft (239m) this is the highest point on the Island.

Leave by following the Shanklin signs to remain on the A3055. A winding ascent (1 in 8) is then made. This passes beneath St Boniface Down with fine sea views to the right, especially from the Landslip.

Later descend (1 in 10). Here you reach the pleasant resort of Shanklin (see page 64). The 'old village' has thatched cottages and one of the prettiest inns on the

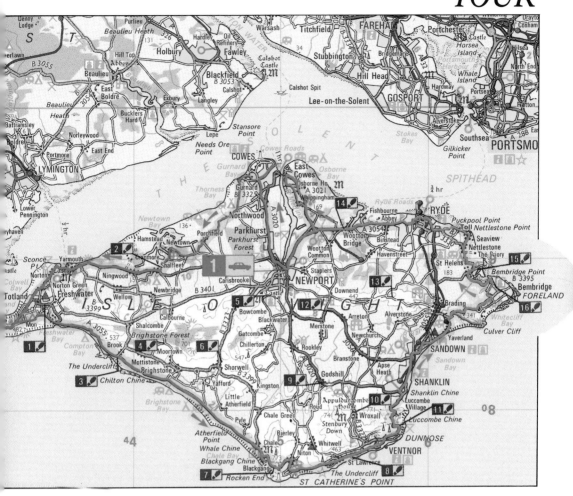

Island, The Crab. Shanklin Chine is a natural gorge of great scenic beauty.

Follow the main road through the town to the residential district of Lake (see page 50). Here pass the Stag Inn and in ¼ mile (400m) bear right at the war memorial. Pass beneath the railway and in just over ½ mile (800m) turn right into Station Avenue (signed Town Centre) to enter Sandown (see page 62). This popular seaside town has an extensive sandy beach and among its attractions are the Isle of Wight Zoo and a local geology museum in the Public Library.

Follow the Bembridge signs to leave by the seafront, B3395. In 1¼ miles (2km) pass 12th-century Yaverland church, and at the T-junction turn right. After another ¼ mile (400m) a detour to the right is available via Bembridge Down (Napoleonic Fort) to reach Culver Down. Here there is an AA Viewpoint and a memorial to the Earl of Yarborough.

The main drive continues along the B3395 and in 1¼ miles (2km) passes Bembridge Airport. Bear left and almost a mile (1.6km) further, at the mini-roundabout, turn left on to an unclassified road. Shortly on the left is the footpath to Bembridge Windmill, built in the early 18th century. Enter the village of Bembridge (see page 37).

From the one-way system, follow the Ryde signs, B3395, and skirt Bembridge Harbour. At St Helens (see page 61) turn right at the T-junction, B3330, signed Nettlestone. In just over ¼ mile (400m) turn left (signed Ryde) and continue to Nettlestone. Here branch right on B3340 (signed Seaview) and almost ¼ mile (400m) further branch right again with an unclassified road, signed Sea Front. The coast is reached again at Seaview (see page 63). Descend the High Street and follow the Esplanade, then keep forward into Bluett Avenue. At the T-junction turn right then keep left along the shoreline. From here there are fine views over Spithead to Portsmouth.

Shortly, pass through a tollgate, passing on the left Oakhill Road. By following this road you reach the Flamingo Park waterfowl and water gardens.

Continue along the coast road, then veer inland and ½ mile (800m) further turn right on to the B3330. Shortly, turn right again with the A3055. Later join the Esplanade to enter Ryde (see page 58). This is the largest resort on the Island and one of the busiest points of entry. The pier is ½ mile (800m) long and the ferry terminal and railway station are at its end. There is a fine beach and excellent views of the Solent.

Follow signs to Newport to leave by the A3054. After 1½ miles (2.4km) pass through Binstead (see page 37) then in 1¼ miles (2km) pass, on the right, the turning to the Fishbourne car ferry. Shortly, enter Wootton Bridge (see page 70), which stands at the head of a creek, and in 1½ miles (2.4km) at the roundabout turn right on to the A3021, signed East Cowes. One mile (1.6km) further turn left on to an unclassified road, signed Whippingham Church. In ½ mile (800m) the road passes Whippingham Church (see page 69). This was built in 1860 for the use of Queen Victoria and her family when they stayed at Osborne House.

Continue for almost a mile (1.6km) and at a T-junction turn left into Victoria Grove. Join Adelaide Grove and at the end turn left again, A3021, into East Cowes (see page 43). This is the busy car ferry terminal which connects with Southampton. A wide variety of craft – including hydrofoils – can be seen, and there is a floating bridge across the River Medina which provides a link with Cowes.

Follow signs Newport (A3054) to leave by the A3021. On the southern outskirts of the town is the entrance to Osborne House (on the left), built in the 19th century in the style of an Italian Renaissance villa. It was for some time the home of Queen Victoria.

Remain on the A3021 and ½ mile (800m) further pass the turning to Barton Manor Vineyard and Gardens (on the left). In 1½ miles (2.4km) at the roundabout take the second exit, A3054, and return to Newport.

WALK 1

Poet's Corner

Allow 3½ hours

This circuit of the Island's western headland provides breathtaking views: from Headon Hill the Solent panorama and The Needles, and from West High Down the remarkable view of the Alum Bay coloured cliffs. The walk along High Down ridge to Tennyson Down is an exhilarating experience. A generally dry walk, but quite exposed.

Starting from the western end of the car park in the centre of Freshwater (SZ337871), take the tarmac path parallel with the road, alongside the stream. Turn right at the T-junction over a small bridge with white rails, and left immediately past the ambulance garage. Follow the tarmac path to the road, bear right, and continue for just over ¾ mile (1.4km) to the T-junction by Totland Parish Church. Cross over and follow York Lane until you reach a further T-junction (Cliff Road). Cross over and take the gravel track and footpath T17 to Headon Warren (NT). Keep straight on over a grassy path, forking right at a seat and right again before the fenced-in summit tumulus. Pause for splendid views of the Solent with Hurst Castle and Lymington River, and the unique Fort Albert, conspicuous on the near shore.

Keep to the obvious path along the ridge and descend slightly to the left at the end. The Needles and the red and white lighthouse come into view, with West High Down above where the original lighthouse stood until 1859.

Bear left along the gravel track before the old fort ruins and descend to the kissing-gate. Bear left to the road. Turn right, and at the entrance to The Needles Hotel and Pleasure Park (toilets here), follow the road round to the left. Take the National Trust road to The Needles Headland, until you reach some chalk steps on the left. Pause before the steps for the best view of the Alum Bay coloured sand cliffs. If heather is blooming, the flanks of Headon Hill present a magnificent picture from here.

Climb the steps, cross the stile at the top, and continue on upwards over the tarmac road, bending left to the summit and a stile by a gate. (If you would like a closer view of The Needles and also the Black Knight rocket site, take the middle tarmac road through the old

fortifications. Return to the stile by the gate.) Bear diagonally left to the top of the ridge and then take a vague path eastwards, descending gradually to another stile and a four-arm signpost before ascending Tennyson Down ahead. To the left of the signpost there is a replica of the old Nodes Beacon which formerly stood on the site of the monument erected to Alfred, Lord Tennyson on the summit in 1897. The panorama from the summit, nearly 500ft (150m) above the sea, gives some of the Island's finest views, from the River Yar, meandering northwards to Yarmouth through its shallow valley, across to the coastline stretching away south-east.

Maintain direction parallel with, but well clear of, the cliff edge on the long gradual descent and final steep section, turning left on to a narrow enclosed lane. Just off the main road (toilets here) turn left along a tarmac path and continue on the road past St Agnes, the thatched church, and post office, taking the left road fork (Bedbury Lane). There is no footpath so beware of traffic. Opposite the gate of Farringford Hotel, formerly the home of Tennyson, take footpath F41 across a field to the road and continue opposite through white posts. If you look to your left here, you will see the old village pound built of flint stones.

Continue along the road to a tarmac path on your right. Follow this round right back to the car park from where you started.

Inlet Outlook

Allow 3 hours

The majority of this walk covers a circuit of a semi-peninsula, bounded on the north by the Solent and on the east and south by tidal inlets off Newtown River. A fair proportion of the route is over dry gravel roads, but this is offset by the intriguing series of catwalks, bridges and

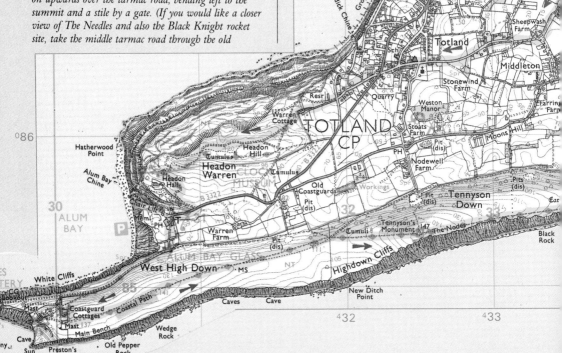

embankments over tidal inlets. A peaceful yet interesting amble but with some muddy spots, particularly after wet weather, so waterproof footwear is advised.

Start from the National Trust car park on Mill Road, Shalfleet (SZ414895). Walk back to the main road, cross over and follow the lane opposite by the church to a T-junction. Turn left. Shalfleet church and its squat Norman tower with walls 5ft (1.5m) thick was built in the 12th century. It was used as a refuge at the time of French invasions of this area during the 14th century.

At the end of the houses, continue round a left-hand bend to a copse and take the path on the right, signed S15 Ningwood. Keep left through the copse and after the first stile cross the field diagonally right by the electricity pole in the centre, and cross a second stile about halfway along the hedge from the copse. Continue in the same direction over the next field to a gate in the corner, turning right along the edge of the adjoining field to reach a gate. Keep to the left edge of the next field and then head for the right side of the house across the next field. When you get there, turn left and then right to the road. (Take care: it is a blind exit on to a fast main road.)

Cross the road and go left for 220yd (200m) to Hamstead Estate Road (signposted) on the right. Follow this road for about ¾ mile (1.3km) and then take the obvious right fork to Creek and Lower Hamstead Farms (S28). At Lower Hamstead Farm continue through the gate towards Newtown River, over the stile on your left.

Turn aside a little to enjoy the river view from the old quay, imagining the time when, some 600 years ago, marauding French ships sailed up to burn and pillage Newtown and the surrounding area.

Follow an enclosed path to a stile on your right and continue along the edge of the tidal inlet and over the footbridge. Take a hairpin turn right over another bridge, go along the slight embankment and then cross further bridges and continue until you reach a stile into a field. Turn right and then left along the side of the field to a stile on your left. Cross the adjoining field diagonally right to the catwalk, continuing along the side of the field to another stile. Take the steps to the beach and turn left. Stretching away north-west is Hamstead Ledge, an outcrop of resistant Bembridge limestone, and particularly strong currents prevail offshore. Before leaving the beachside, look left and you will see a small stone memorial to three young men lost at sea locally in 1932 and 1934.

Follow the track, diverging away from the beach upwards to Hamstead Farm. Shortly after diverging, you will see a concrete ramp to the beach, a remnant of wartime when tanks landed here. Before the farm there are fine views of the Newtown River complex where fingers of water feel their way through Hamstead clays.

Continue past the farm on the main track, which soon bends to pass Hamstead Grange which can be seen on the left. Follow the road back to the stone bridge and shortly after it take the signposted path left (S11), following it round right to the footbridge. Keeping the hedge on your left, follow the boundaries of two fields to the main road. Turn left and walk back along the verge to Shalfleet village and the car park from where the walk started.

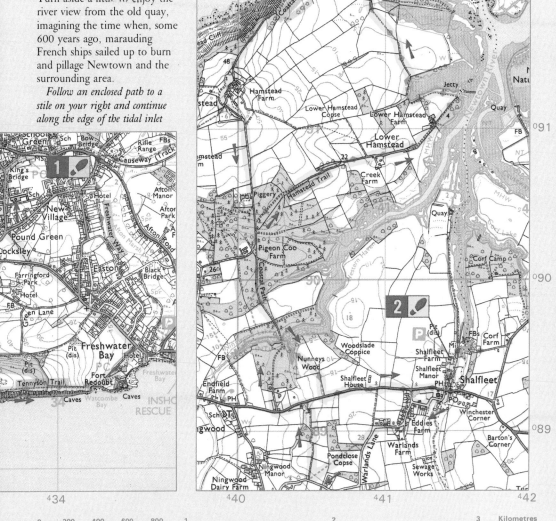

A Trip round the Bay

Allow 3 hours

The first half of this walk affords views of the coastline dominated by the distant Tennyson Down with the monument to its namesake on the summit. The return is over the ancient highway along the downland ridge. Not a walk for wet and windy days.

Start from the National Trust car park on the Military Road at Brook (SZ385835). Leave by the beach gate, taking the path along the bank on the right. Join the cliff-top path over the stile and follow this westwards, keeping a safe distance from the eroding cliff edge. Pause at the stile and look back to Brook Green and notice the roofless shell of the old lifeboat house, a relic of days when Brook was an important lifeboat station on this hazardous, smuggler-inhabited coast.

After about ½ mile (0.9km), cross Shippards Chine car park (toilets at the road entrance), continuing westwards on the obvious cliff path. Compton Bay is a popular beach and the haunt of surfers. Severe erosion problems are obvious over the next ¾ mile (1.2km), acres of fields having slumped seawards within living memory.

Reach the stile and paths to the beach and road. Follow the road path as it bears round right, mount the left hand bank and continue along the cliff. After crossing over Compton Chine stream, look for the steps to the roadside as you climb the slope. At this point the sandstone cliffs give way to chalk. On descending to cross the chine stream, note the route of the old sunken highway ahead on the side of the down and its crossing over the existing road to disappear at the cliff edge.

At the top of the steps turn left, crossing the road in 220yd (200m) to the bridleway over the sunken track diverging away from the road. Follow to the point where it converges with the chalk track (at a sign board). Take the hairpin turn right and follow the obvious track over Afton Down through the golf course. Pause at the hairpin to take in the splendid views. To the north is the River Yar valley, with Yarmouth and the Solent beyond. To the north-west lie the low white ramparts of Golden Hill Fort, and jutting out from the far shore, Hurst Castle where Charles I was held prisoner before being taken to Westminster and the block.

Continue on the obvious chalk track, passing through a gate to maintain the same direction over the grass track through the gorse scrub. Keep to the right of the knoll and the National Trust plinth, continuing around the side of the down to descend to the double power line post immediately ahead. As you descend, notice Brook Hill House, once the home of J B Priestley, set in the forest across the valley. At one time it was marked as a fortress on German war maps but it survived hostilities, only to suffer the onslaught of students and weather before being sold and converted into flats. Its gutted shell now stands like the bridge of a ship. The old highway can also be clearly seen continuing up over Chessell Down opposite.

Take a hairpin right turn just before the power line post and follow the rough track, keeping the power lines on the left. Shortly after the point where the power lines are overhead, diverge left through a gate to the signpost. Turn left at BS86A to follow the good track, descending to cross the tarmac access road on to the grass track between the fence and hedge (bridleway BS52). After 440yd (400m) turn right along the broad enclosed track and then left at the pair of stone cottages. Follow to the T-junction with the narrow lane by a white house and maintain this direction over the stile opposite Military Road and your starting point a short distance to your left.

The Barrows and the Longstone

Allow 2¾ hours

The village of Brighstone is tucked under the downland ridge in the centre of the south-west coastal shelf, and this is a walk along part of that ridge with a descent through beautiful woodland to Brighstone. Bronze Age and Neolithic burial mounds are passed on the way, and the climb back to Brighstone Down provides superb panoramic views of the south-west. Good walking but as there are some muddy sections after rain, stout footwear is advised.

Start from the National Trust car park on the Calbourne to Brighstone road (SZ420846) and take the obvious path westwards to the summit of Mottistone Down. Splendid views unfold and on the summit you will see four Bronze Age barrows or burial mounds which adjoined the local community of Harboro, circa 1500BC.

Pass straight over and descend to the gate. After it, take the first forest ride left and then left again. Follow the broad grassy track along the contour of the down, gradually descending to a T-junction on a gravel track Turn left round the edge of the woods and continue the short distance to the Longstone. The two stones – one standing, the other lying – have been the subject of many dramatic and mystical theories, but the true archaeological explanation is that they stood at the end of a Neolithic long barrow or burial mound, the site probably being used as a moot or meeting place in medieval times.

Cross the stile in the fence ahead and keep straight on over a further stile and a track to the road. Turn right and soon after take the path to the left running up a gravel track to the woods. Cross the stile and turn right along a broad grassy track. The track gets narrower as it descends and bends gradually right to emerge at the south-east corner of the woods. (Ignore footpaths leading right into the woods.) Cross a stile and walk along the edge of the field to a further stile and take a narrow path that descends to the lane. Turn right and in about 130yd (120m), after a slight bend, take an inconspicuous path left (BS64) and follow this to the road, where you turn left. After a further 130yd (120m) take a path right (BS39) to Moortown Lane. Turn left and then take a hairpin right turn into Upper Lane. Ignore Hollis Drive to the left and continue for 880yd (800m) or so to the first road junction and take bridleway BS81 left. At this point you can choose to deviate into Brighstone village, where the post office, pub, and toilets are all within 3 minutes' walk. In days gone by, Brighstone was a noted smuggling village. It also boasted the first Isle of Wight lifeboat, but the area is now covered by Yarmouth. The coxswain of Brighstone's first lifeboat was James Buckett, a reformed smuggler who had just served five years compulsory duty in the navy for his crimes.

The church is an outstanding building dating from 1190. The most interesting source of historical information about the church and village is in the parish books, which prior to 1588 mention preparations at the village to combat the increasing threat of the Spanish Armada.

Follow an enclosed track upwards, bearing round right to the top of the down. As you climb, pause for splendid views of the coastal plain, from Blackgang Bluff in the east to the Tennyson cliffs in the west, with Brighstone sprawling in the foreground.

Continue over the top of the down on a grassy path, and turn left at the T-junction to follow the broad track along the edge of a large field, to the gate. Pass through this and maintain direction, by bearing round to the left on the obvious track up to the top of the down and a field-gate. Turn left, follow the track to the road and cross to the car park from where the walk started.

SCALE 1:25 000

WALK 5

Carisbrooke Castle from near and far

Allow 3½ hours

This walk is dominated by views of Carisbrooke Castle, from close up on the ramparts to distant views high above the Bowcombe Valley. The Newport and River Medina panorama is worth 5 minutes deviation shortly after starting, and the closing stages through quiet water meadows are in contrast to the high ridge of Bowcombe Down. Stout footwear is advised as some parts can be muddy after rain. Please close all gates as sheep and cattle are grazing in some of the fields.

Begin at the car park on Whitcombe Road, Carisbrooke (SZ489876). There are splendid views from here of the southern ramparts of Carisbrooke Castle, where Charles I was imprisoned.

Cross the road to the narrow lane on the south side of St Dominic's Priory. Shortly after the end of the perimeter wall, take footpath N26 left, following the track to the cemetery wall. If you turn aside to the right for a few minutes you can walk to the end of the wall and enjoy the view of Newport and the River Medina from Mount Joy. On descending, the television masts of Chillerton (left) and Rowridge (right) are clearly visible.

Return following the cemetery wall and the steps to the road. Turn left and almost immediately right, following the path by the gate to the Castle, bearing left along the southern ramparts above the moat. Follow the path round to the right and at the car park turn sharp left and almost immediately right to descending path N88. If you turn off to the right when you enter

the car park, you can see the gates of Carisbrooke Castle.

Bear right on reaching a narrow lane and take the left fork (Clatterford Shute) over a ford to the main road. Cross right into Nodgham Lane and shortly after the top of the rise take an inconspicuous hairpin turn left into Down Lane (Tennyson Trail). Follow the enclosed track for about 1 mile (1.6km) to a metal gate. On this section, look back in an open stretch for a fine view of Carisbrooke Castle. Below is Bowcombe Valley and Chillerton ITV mast.

Continue in the same direction through a gate (bridleway N128), turning diagonally left through a further gate at the end of the field. Pass along an enclosed track and through two more gates. Pause at the second gate for views of the Solent to the north, with Newtown estuary to the left and the chimneys of Fawley oil refinery on the far shore.

Continue to the next gate and a five-way signpost. Turn left along an enclosed track (N135) and when the track bends right take a field track forking left following the electric power lines. Ahead, slightly to the right through a gap in the hills, the chalk Culver Cliffs can be seen.

After the next gate take the right fork and go on to another gate, then follow a chalky track to the road. Cross diagonally left (bridleway N137a), running along the field edge to the gate. Maintain direction along the edge of the next field to a gate on your right. Pass through the gate and turn left along a broad chalky track to a T-junction. Turn left along a track towards Bowcombe Farm. Just before the farmhouse, turn right along an enclosed lane, and right again at the next T-junction near Plaish Farm. Follow this lane for a short while and then take the stile on your left along the side of the long water meadows. Keep going until you reach the stepping stones and a lane. Turn right along the lane and keep right at the bend and a path junction. Follow the tarmac lane over the ford, bearing left at Froglands Farm to the main road and the car park ahead on your left.

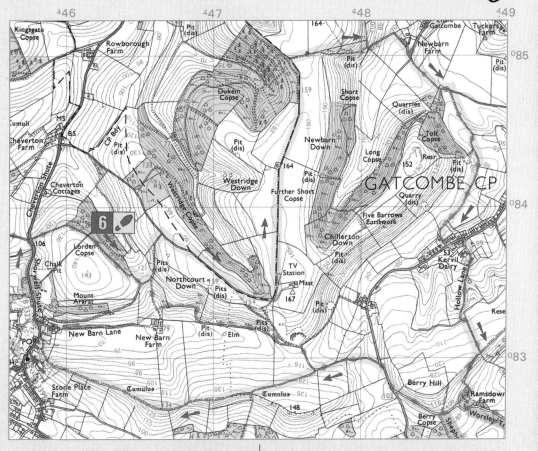

The TV Mast Circuit

Allow 3¼ hours

This walk hardly loses sight of Chillerton Down television mast and includes close-ups under the massive stay wires. The mast is 750ft (230m) high and was erected in 1958. A unique start in beautiful surroundings is quickly left for the first stiff climb, but the breathtaking views soon make it worth while. Stout footwear is advised.

Start from the small car park on Shorwell Shute (SZ458835), turning left to take the path ascending on your left (SW57). After the top of the rise, go down the steps on the right and cross the footbridge. The original bridge, built in the 18th century, carried owners of nearby Northcourt House to a summer house in the woods.

Turn right and within a short distance take the path that diverges left and follow it around the perimeter of the Dell to the far northern end. On the slight rise from the footbridge, view Northcourt House left and walk over the indistinct foundations of an old summer house, the floor of which was paved with sheep's knuckle bones.

Cross the stile and walk up the right side of the field to a stile at the top of the bank. Go on to a further stile, where you turn left and then right to the road. Cross (carefully) to the track opposite (signed Bridle Road to Chillerton) and continue, keeping the wood on your left. You will see some fine views of Bowcombe Valley from this section.

Shortly after the copse ends, turn left through a gate and, keeping left through a separate gate, follow the chalky track up to a concrete road. Turn right, and follow the road to the TV mast entrance. Turn left through the gate following the waymark along the right side of the field, passing through a barn complex on your way to a wood. Soon after passing the mast, look right to Sandown Bay and Culver Cliffs.

Follow the woodland track for about 330yd (300m) and then turn right at the second turning (signpost G22) to the bridlegate. Continue along the left side of the field. Shortly after a further gate, drop down right to turn left on an obvious track. Descend to the gate and track to New Barn Farm, turning right to reach the farm entrance road. Turn right and continue over a field track ahead on your right (G6). Pass through a gate, go straight ahead for 55yd (50m), then take the track on your right (G6) to Chillerton along the side of a field. Continue in the same direction along the left edge of two further fields and then go down an enclosed track to the road at Chillerton. Turn left, and before a telephone box take the rough road right (G15a) Hollow Lane, following the enclosed track upwards. When you reach a T-junction turn left, and then right at a second T-junction, on to a good track descending to Ramsdown Farm. On the way down there is a fine view.

Turn right on to the road and right again when you get to a T-junction. After 220yd (200m) take the track on your left (G13) and follow it upwards to a left-hand track marked BR to Shorwell. Here continue ahead along the right of the field and enclosed section, until you emerge on a ridge on the left of a field. Continue along the whole length of the ridge and over a stile. Follow the track as it swings round right and drops steeply to a further stile and a gate to the road. Along the ridge there are views out to sea.

Turn right along the road and you will soon come to the car park and finish point. Turn left for the post office, church and pub.

WALK 7
The Three Lighthouses

Allow 2 hours (or 3, including the Hoy's Monument extension)

The walk starts by looking down on St Catherine's Lighthouse then goes inland to its 14th-century predecessor, the Oratory or 'Pepper Pot' on St Catherine's Hill. Nearby is the 'Salt Cellar', an 18th-century lighthouse never completed. Before setting out it is worth reading the Heritage Coast information in the car park.

Park in the viewpoint car park above Blackgang (SZ491767). Go up the steps at the back of the car park by Hawks Ledge and follow the path to the seat on the cliff-top promontory. Note the view from here across the bays.
Turn left along the cliff-top path towards Niton.

St Catherine's Lighthouse, you see below, was completed in 1840 following the tragic wreck of the *Clarendon* in Chale Bay when all passengers and all but three of the crew were lost. The lighthouse greatly reduced the number of shipwrecks – prior to its building as many as 14 wrecks occurred in Chale Bay in one night. The land surrounding the lighthouse (Knowles Farm) is owned by the National Trust and you will notice that it is almost unique among Island farms in that the field boundaries are stone walls instead of hedges. The stone was readily available in the form of debris slipped from the cliff above and using it for walls was economical as well as helping to clear the fields for cultivation.

After the second stile beyond the radio station, turn immediately left over another stile and head inland, keeping the fence and sparse hedge on your right. At the far end of the field cross a stile and branch slightly left, as waymarked, to a further stile in a hollow 55yd (50m) on. After crossing this stile descend to the road, turn right, and follow it round to Niton church. Turn left at the lych gate and go up Pan Lane. At the end of the road go straight up bridleway NT53, signposted to St Catherine's Down. Bury Lane probably takes its name from the Bronze Age barrow that used to stand near the top before it was ploughed out. The old name for a barrow was a 'hury'.

Turn left at the top and follow the track to the gate. Go through and continue along the track ahead, as indicated by the blue arrow, to the next gate and cattle-grid. Pass through the gate then turn immediately left and follow the fence-line uphill to the Oratory.

Alternatively, branch half right across the field to the gate and, keeping to the left-hand fork, follow the ridge leading north to Hoy's Monument. Return by the same route, and then climb to the Oratory. This diversion is worth while for the fine views on either side. The history of the Oratory, and the later attempt to build another lighthouse nearby, is given on the National Trust information board by the tower. (See 'Flotsam, Jetsam and Lagan', page 22).

Cross the stile leading out of the Oratory enclosure and head across the field towards the sea to a stile on the far side midway between two telegraph poles. Cross this stile and branch slightly left, as waymarked, and descend the well-trodden path across the next two fields straight towards the car park, now clearly visible.

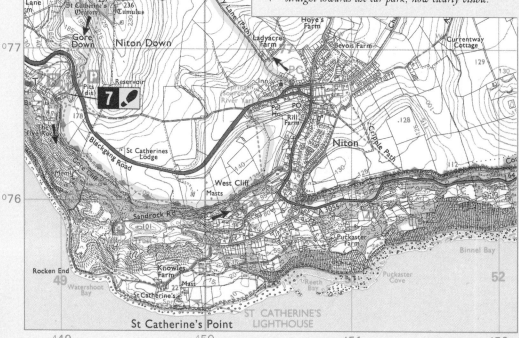

Under Cliff and Over Cliff

Allow 1¾ hours

An enchanting walk through the romantic St Lawrence Undercliff, returning along the clifftop. A separate tour beforehand of the Botanic Gardens is well worth while. Although the walk is fairly short, there is a steady climb halfway and a steep descent towards the end. Where the path follows the cliff-edge keep an eye on children and pets.

Park in the Ventnor Botanic Gardens car park (SZ547769). Leave the western end of the car park, passing the temperate house, and follow the sign pointing across the meadow to the coastal footpath. The Undercliff is a result of the porous Greensand rock sliding down towards the sea on a layer of underlying Gault Clay.

Pass Orchard Bay House and, keeping the sea on your left, follow the coastal footpath for the next ⅝ mile (1km) to the old coastguard cottages at Woody Bay. Keep to the seaward side of the cottages and about 220yd (200m) past them turn inland up footpath V97, signposted to St Lawrence. About 55yd (50m) past the signpost turn left off the farm track, keeping the fence on your left and the sea behind you. Cross the stile and climb the steep path to Wolverton Road. The road takes its name from the property just to the east, which has in its private garden the ruin of a 14th-century house built by the de Wolvertons.

Turn left along Wolverton Road then right up to the main road. Cross over and go up Spindlers Road, turn left along Seven Sisters Road, then right up the footpath signposted to Whitwell and Niton. Known at St Rhadegund's Path, these steps are part of the ancient route between St Lawrence and Whitwell, where the church is dedicated to Saints Mary and Rhadegund.

Climb the steps to the top and turn right along the path towards Ventnor. After 600yd (550m) go over the stile down the bank to the road at St Lawrence Shute, climb up the other side, and turn right along the path towards Ventnor. Follow the fenced-in path and near the end of the first field turn right down footpath V76, signposted to St Lawrence. Descend the rough steps built through a cleft in the rock. The 'shelves' in the Greensand cliff are formed by harder bands of a rock called Chert which are left protruding as the wind and rain erode the soft sandstone in between.

Follow the steps down to the right and continue down the winding path to a metal kissing-gate followed closely by another. These gates mark the site of a level crossing on the old railway from Ventnor to Newport which closed in 1952.

After the second kissing-gate, descend the winding path into Pelham Wood and when you see the houses in front of you, join the estate road by the green signpost. Turn right down the road to the main Undercliff Drive. Turn left for 55yd (50m), cross over, and go down footpath V92, signposted to Orchard Bay. When it joins the road turn left across the meadow back to the Botanic Gardens.

An 1860 engraving which shows Ventnor prior to its rapid expansion into a popular seaside resort

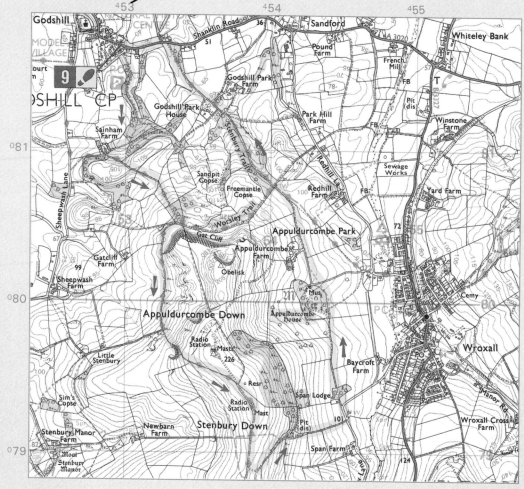

Appuldurcombe Trail

Allow 2½ hours (3½ if you visit the House)

A steady climb through woods and farmland to the magnificent views of Stenbury Down, returning via the 18th-century mansion of Appuldurcombe House.

Park at Godshill car park (SZ530817), cross the main road, go up the narrow road opposite and turn left over the stile behind the Griffin, signposted to Beech Copse. Follow the stiles to Beech Copse and on entering the wood bear right, with the ditch on your left. Cross the ditch on the sleeper footbridge and climb the steep bank to the bridleway on top. Despite its name, the predominant tree species in the wood is chestnut, planted to provide fence posts. Now seldom used for this purpose, the trees have been allowed to grow towards maturity and in November the nuts provide rich pickings. In May the woodland floor is covered with bluebells.

Turn right along the bridleway leading out of the copse and continue ahead to Sainham Farm. Cross the stile and follow footpath GL56 through the white gate and turn left up footpath GL58, signposted to Gatcliff. Follow the track uphill, along the level, then round to the right up the next hill, with the hedge on your left. Follow the track into the copse then turn right at the signpost and follow bridleway GL49, signposted to

Stenbury Down. Keep the stone wall on your left for the next mile (1.6km) and climb to the top of Stenbury Down, emerging on to the roadway by a cattle-grid. This wall, originally 6ft (1.8m) high, was built 250 years ago to enclose Appuldurcombe Park and prevent the deer from escaping into surrounding farmland.

Turn right passing the radio station and follow the road as it bends round to the left and descends to the foot of the down. At the T-junction opposite the cottages, turn left, leave the road at the corner and walk into the farmyard, passing Span Lodge on your left. Pass the barn and keep straight ahead along the track until you reach the rear entrance to Appuldurcombe House. The House (open daily) was built in 1710 by Sir Robert Worsley on the site of a Tudor mansion. It was once described as the finest private residence on the Island, but it is now only a shell. During its history the House has served as a school, a refuge for exiled French monks, and a billet for troops. Its demise came in World War II when it was severely damaged by a landmine; an echo of the gunpowder explosion in the gatehouse that killed two sons of an earlier Richard Worsley.

Keeping the railings on your left, follow the footpath round the edge of the grounds and emerge on to the farm road by the main entrance to the House. With your back to the main gates, follow the farm road ahead, go past Appuldurcombe Farm on your left, then follow the edge of the field to the three arches of the Freemantle Gate. This Ionic triumphal arch was the main gate to Appuldurcombe from Godshill, and was reputedly designed by James Wyatt.

Pass through, continue ahead downhill past Godshill Park Farm, and go straight on to join the main road. Turn left back to the car park.

Wroxall Downs

Allow 2½ hours

It is best to choose a clear day for this walk if you can, as the views across the Island and out to sea are superb.

Park in the car park in Station Approach, Wroxall (SZ551799), near the church. Leave the car park and walk up Station Road past the school. At the top of the hill, branch right over the stile opposite Castle Lane and follow the V30 footpath uphill. Cross two more stiles, then keep to the left-hand edge of the next field, ignoring the path that descends to the lower level. On the far side of this field you reach the site of 'Cook's Castle'. All that now remains is some raised ground in the corner of the field but this was once a mock ruin, built to be viewed from Appuldurcombe House (which you can see to the west) when the landscape was fashioned by Capability Brown.

Cross a stile, continue ahead for 220yd (200m), then turn right over a stile under a larch tree. Turn left and follow the edge of the field for 45yd (41m), then turn right to cross the field uphill to a bridlegate in the fence on the far side. Pass through and continue uphill, following the left-hand lip of the old quarry. On the top side, branch left round the contour, following bridleway V45, signposted to Luccombe Down. Pass through a bridlegate then continue straight ahead to a signpost on the skyline. On reaching it, turn right and follow bridleway V40. Keeping the hedge on your left, pass through a gateway and continue straight ahead along this bridleway, which becomes V43. From this path you can see both ends of the Island: Culver Cliff in the east and The Needles in the west.

At the far end of the long field pass through the gate and continue ahead along the flinty track through gorse.

This is a designated Site of Special Scientific Interest. The chalk is capped by a very acid flinty soil supporting the large area of heather (a comparative rarity on the Island), and the gorse is a breeding site for the rare Dartford warbler.

Keep to this track (ignoring the left turn) until you reach the boundary fence of the radar station. Turn right and follow the track (becoming a road) with the radar station fence on your left. About 220yd (200m) past the radar station turn right down bridleway V8, signposted to Wroxall, descend steeply through Wroxall Copse, and follow the bridleway straight downhill to Wroxall Manor Farm. This was an important manor at the time of the Domesday Survey in 1086 and was valued at £20. The house has changed little since 1770 and the exceptionally long barn is particularly interesting.

Pass through the farmyard out on to the road and turn left, following the road to the Star Inn. Go straight down the High Street, up the other side towards the church, and turn right at the newsagent back to the car park.

Appuldurcombe House and grounds in their heyday

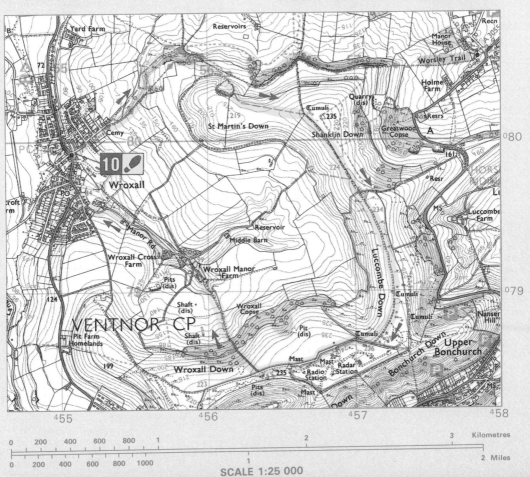

WALK *11*
Luccombe Landslip

Allow 1¼ hours

An enchanting little walk, not to be missed. It is quite short but you should allow plenty of time to appreciate the beautiful scenery. For the very energetic walker there is a further steep descent through Luccombe Chine to the beach, returning by the same route, in which case allow another ½ hour or so.

The romantic rock-garden village of Bonchurch lies at the foot of St Boniface and Bonchurch Downs

Park at Nansen Hill (the Landslip) car park by the picnic site (SZ581789). Enter the grounds of Smugglers' Haven tea gardens, pass across the lawn in front of the café, then turn left down the steps by the shelter. Turn right and follow the winding path with the stone wall on your left. Descend the Devil's Chimney steps through a cleft in the rock. This split in the rock probably occurred when the Landslip was formed in 1810, when a huge land mass collapsed towards the sea forming the undercliff into which you are descending.

Continue down the steps through the trees. Halfway down ignore the side paths and continue down the steps to the shelter in the Lower Landslip. Turn left along the footpath signposted to Luccombe and Shanklin. To the left of the path are huge ivy-clad boulders that tumbled down from the sandstone cliff in the great land movement. A little further on, look hard and you will see one marked Wishing Seat, on which generations of children have sat and made a wish. To the right are some particularly ancient oak trees twisted into fantastic shapes. One of these has grown out of a cleft in a huge boulder and its roots now engulf the rock; others have ferns growing from their gnarled branches.

At the far end of the Landslip by Loafer's Glory continue straight on to Dunnose Cottage. About 110yd (100m) past the cottage turn left at the narrow road. (At this point you may turn right down Luccombe Chine to the beach, then return to the same spot.) If you make this diversion, imagine what life must have been like for the families of fishermen who used to occupy five cottages at the foot of the Chine until they had to move out in the 1890s because of subsidence. The Chine was undoubtedly a route for smugglers, and the rocks to the north are called Johnny New, after a man who used to sink his contraband there.

About 55yd (50m) up the road branch right over the stile by the National Trust sign, and walk up across the field towards the little red-roofed barn of Luccombe Farm. Cross the stile to the left of the barn, turn left, and follow the track with the hedge on your left until you reach the narrow road by the white-painted Luccombe Farm Cottages. Go straight across and follow the steep footpath to the right of the cottages, signposted to Bonchurch, and climb the steps back to the main road. Turn left and return to the car park.

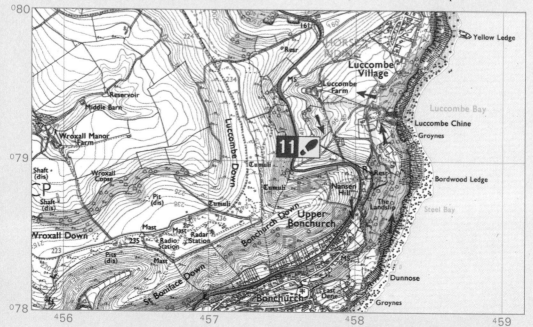

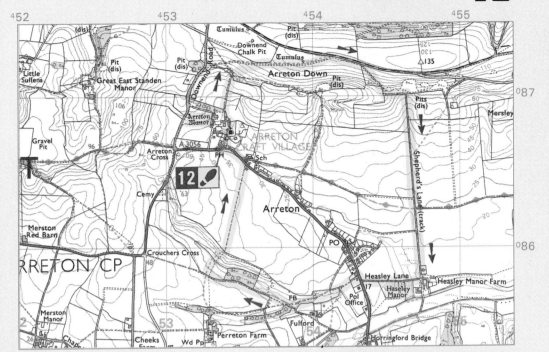

From Fertile Valley to Hidden Vale

Wordsworth's 'ethereal minstrel', the popular skylark

Allow 2 hours (excluding visits to the manors)

This walk passes two manor houses and an ancient church. There are superb views from Arreton Down over the Island's most fertile valley, and towards the end of the walk you go through a hidden vale which in early summer is yellow with flag irises.

Park on the verge opposite the White Lion pub (SZ534867). Cross the road and proceed to the church (worth a visit) behind the pub. Follow footpath A12, signposted to the downs. After the farm buildings, keep the fence on your right, passing the rear entrance to Arreton Manor. The Manor, which dates from 1612, has a fascinating history and is now open to the public, but watch out for the ghost!

Continue uphill and near the top of the field branch right up some steps and over a stile. Continue diagonally across the hillside, passing the electricity pole on your right. Pass close to the south-east corner of the quarry fence then continue on the same diagonal route, aiming for a tall electricity pole behind the roadside hedge on the skyline.

Strike the road by signpost A11, turn right, and follow the roadside fence for 270yd (247m). Branch right down bridleway A17, signposted to Haseley Manor (do not continue along the roadside path). Follow the sunken lane diagonally downhill, bend round to the left, and descend to the metal gate on your right (if this part of the route is muddy, follow the left-hand bank). Turn right through the gateway marked by the blue arrow, and follow the dead straight Shepherd's Lane to Haseley Manor. The lane is the old drive to Haseley, a manor house, parts of which date from Norman times. It was almost derelict in 1976 when the present owners bought and restored it. The Manor and pottery studio (with hourly demonstrations) are open to the public every day except Christmas Day.

Turn right at the Manor gates and follow the access road until you reach the main road. Cross over and follow the footpath diagonally opposite by Arbutus Cottage. Enter the field behind the houses and go straight across to the stile on the far side, then continue along the edge of the next field as waymarked, with the fence on your right. After 80yd (73m), where another path joins from the right, fork left and follow the trodden path gently downhill through the marshy field. Cross the second ditch on the concrete bridge, then bear right uphill to a gate. Pass through and follow the blue arrow along the broad grassy track with a bank on your left and a valley on your right. Pass through the next gate and continue along the bridleway with the copse on your right.

Turn right 190yd (174m) past the end of the copse, where there is a gap in the bank, and walk down across the field to the stream on the far side. Cross the stream on the culvert and go straight up the steep hill to the stile at the top. Cross the wide open field by following the direction (straight ahead) indicated by the HT waymark (usually well trodden). Strike the road by the community centre, cross over, and turn left back to the White Lion.

SCALE 1:25 000

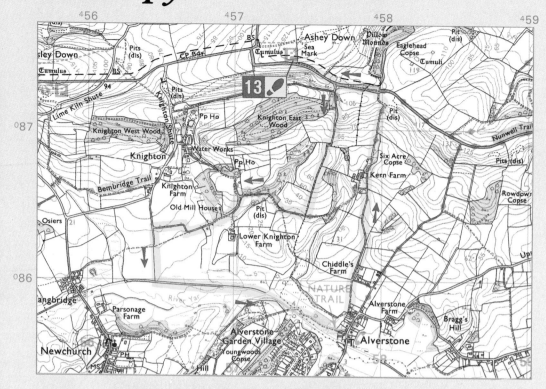

The Tranquil Yar Valley

The big-footed coot has an ungainly 'Max Wall' walk

Allow 2 hours

A gentle walk into the quiet valley of the River Yar, where it is excellent for bird-watching. Wear stout shoes as parts of the walk may be muddy after rain.

Park in the car park below Ashey Down (SZ574874). Cross the road from the car park and turn left along the roadside path to the bridleway sign. Turn right through the metal gate and continue straight ahead down the bridleway, ignoring NC4 on your right. In just over ½ mile (0.8km) you reach a T-junction with another track. This valley has been inhabited since prehistoric times, as frequent finds of stone tools

prove. It was also an important settlement in medieval days, and the field below you is still called 'vineyard' by local people – a verbal record of a long-forgotten use. The valley is now one of Britain's major producers of sweet corn and garlic.

Turn right along the track and keep to the right, passing the entrance to the sandpit on your right. Follow the sandy path past the plantation and at the next junction fork left towards Newchurch. When the track joins the road turn slightly right and follow it over a little bridge. To your left at Lower Knighton Farm you can see an 18th-century weather-boarded granary supported by staddle stones. These stones, which look like toadstools, kept vermin and damp from reaching the grain.

Continue along the road and 160yd (146m) past the dog-leg, turn left down the bridleway signposted to Alverstone, and when it joins the old railway track turn left again towards Alverstone. This is part of the old Sandown to Newport line which closed in 1956. The Island once had 56 miles (89km) of railway, but in the 1950s they were cut by more than half as trade was lost to the more convenient bus services. Further closures in the 1960s left only the stretch from Ryde to Shanklin open.

Pass the black iron bridge, and in 220yd (200m) branch left over the stile and follow the riverside path to the old Alverstone Mill. The Mill is now a private house, but it ground corn from Domesday times (when it was valued at 40 pence) until 1950.

Turn left up the road and after 160yd (150m) turn left along the footpath by the old school. Turn right after the last house, up the path with a garden on your right, go through a metal gate, and keeping the fence on your left follow the edge of the field to join the road by a stone barn. Continue ahead up the road towards the downs. Near the bungalow go straight ahead by the bridleway signposted to Ashey Down. Pass Kern Farm on your left, go through the metal gate, and continue ahead towards the downs along the farm track. At the top of the downs go through the gate and turn immediately left along the Downland Way path parallel to the road, and follow this back until you reach the car park.

Creekside and Monastery

Allow 2¾ hours

The upper reaches of Wootton Creek are fed by a brook running from the central downland ridge. This walk runs parallel with the west side of the creek and returns via a monastery. Stout footwear is advisable.

From the car park in Brannon Way off Wootton High Street (SZ544919) walk down High Street, turning right at the bottom into Lakeside Holiday Centre. Inside the entrance, fork right passing Fernhill Farm, on a good gravel track through pleasant woodland and fields to the railway crossing. Beware of rolling-stock. Cross over and through the yard of Woodhouse Farm, continuing on the gravel track to the T-junction. Turn left to Great Briddlesford, passing round the pond and through the gate on to the enclosed track, which you follow to the road. Turn left and follow the road, passing under the railway arch and shortly after, the bridge over Blackbridge Brook. On the left above the railway arch is the Isle of Wight Railway Centre at Havenstreet Station, now a mecca for steam enthusiasts.

Shortly after crossing the brook take the track to the right just before the garage (footpath R8), and follow it to the end. Maintain this direction over the stile, along the edge of the field to the twin stiles, and in a short

distance turn left over another stile to the road ahead. Continue in this direction, turning right at the next two T-junctions. Shortly after Havenstreet Post Office at the right-hand bend, continue straight ahead to the stile and climb the grassy hill, keeping to the right of the war memorial shrine on the summit. South are fine views of the central downland ridge and northwards the sea is visible with the mainland beyond.

Maintain this direction over the stile and down a long field to a further stile, crossing the narrow meadow and going through the gate to Newnham Farm ahead. Follow the concrete track to the road, maintaining this direction to the bend, where you take the stile on the left. On footpath R4, cross the field as indicated, keeping left of the largest and nearest oak, and enter the wood by the inconspicuous bridge, bearing right to follow the worn path through the wood to the stile and field. Pass along the left side of the field to the road and cross to the track opposite. (Beware of fast-moving traffic.) Follow to the T-junction and turn left along the wide gravel track. A short trip to the right enables the remains of the old Cistercian Abbey of Quarr to be seen, and shortly after turning left you will pass under an old stone archway. The fine modern Abbey built of red brick lies ahead to the right.

Pass over the crossing and maintain this direction to the road where you turn left. At the telephone box on the right take the footpath R1 to the T-junction and turn left along the private road to the bend. Continue ahead, descending to the concrete bridge over the brook, and climb to the main road. Turn right to Wootton Bridge and on to the car park.

WALK 15

Around Seaview

Allow 3 hours

The unique St Helens Duver provides a good
starting point for this walk which takes in the
villages of St Helens and Seaview, some pleasant
countryside, and a seawall walk. Good walking
but there are some muddy areas after rain.

*Start from the National Trust car park, The Duver, St
Helens (SZ637892), and leave by the interpretation
board. Cross the road and, keeping to the right of the
bushes ahead, follow the vague track past a National
Trust collection box to the old Mill Dam wall. St
Helens Duver was the site of the Royal Isle of
Wight Golf Club from 1882 until 1961, when it
was handed to the National Trust. Its dune-like soil
supports over 250 flora species.*

*Cross the Dam wall and turn right past a caravan
site up Mill Road to St Helens Green. Turn left along
Lower Green Road, bearing right across the green to the
Vine Inn on Upper Green Road. Take the concrete path
at the side of the Inn, maintaining direction through a
small housing development, bearing slightly right to
follow an enclosed path by the school playing-field to the
main road.*

*Turn left, and at the right-hand bend continue ahead
on the track signed R63. Follow this for ½ mile
(0.5km) to a downhill right bend and leave the track to
continue ahead through the gateway. Follow the obvious
track skirting a hedge on the left to the far side of the
field and the junction with a signpost. Turn right along
an enclosed track (B12) to Park Farm. Maintain
direction through the yard, keeping the house on your
left, to the access drive. Descend into a hollow and shortly*

*after the drive rises, and 100yd (91m) beyond the sign
R62, take an enclosed track right (R61). Follow this
track to the end and maintain direction along the field
edge. Pass through a small gate and cross or go round
the paddock to the far right-hand corner and two gates
to the private access drive. Maintain direction to the
road and turn left to the Wishing Well pub. Take the
broad track that passes in front of the pub (R59), which
narrows before turning and reaching the road at
Flamingo Park. Turn right and descend the hill to the
sea-front, and right again along the vehicle toll road.
Across Spithead, Portsmouth is clearly visible, as
are two of four sea-forts built between 1860 and
1880 to deter French invasion.*

*As the road turns right into Salterns Road, continue
ahead along the seawall walk to the road where, at
Hayward House, you turn left along Seaview
Esplanade, enter High Street and take the third left
(Pier Road). Fork right opposite the last house on the
seaward side, and follow the road to its end, continuing
over a narrow path to Seagrove Bay. Turn right along
Fernclose Road (signed R74) and the gravel track
beyond. At the far end by a stone cottage turn left along
an enclosed track and then right over a private drive,
past the Holiday Centre entrance. Go through the
kissing-gate on your left (R85) to the footbridge and
stile at the bottom of the sloping meadow. Turn left
along the side of the field to a stile in the far left corner.
Cross into Duver Road opposite and follow this back to
the car park. Before crossing, deviate left to see the
remains of 12th-century St Helens Church.*

Sea Breezes

Allow 3 hours, including ½ hour for a visit to the windmill (open in summer only)

An easy walk around the perimeter of Bembridge, including the Island's only remaining windmill. There is plenty of sea air and some woodland too.

Park in the car park by the Royal Spithead Hotel (SZ642887). Go up the gravel road opposite the Pilot Boat Inn, signposted Coastal Path BB33 Foreland, and at the junction with the unmade road turn left towards the sea then right along footpath BB6, signposted to Foreland. The water drawn from a well here has remarkable properties and in earlier centuries the Navy would anchor offshore to replenish water supplies, which were said to keep fresh for a voyage round the world.

Follow the wooded track past the Sailing Club start butt; then the path joins the top of the shingle bank. Follow the shingle bank, then the seawall as far as the Lifeboat Station. Bembridge Ledge has always been treacherous to shipping, claiming hundreds of lives over the centuries, and a lifeboat has been stationed here since 1867.

Leaving the Lifeboat Station car park, walk along the seaward edge of the green, turn right, passing the entrance to the Chalet Hotel, and follow the footpath between fences. Turn left along the gravel road signposted Coastal Path, turn right at Forelands Farm, passing Paddock Drive, turn left along Beachfield Road (signposted Coastal Path) and at the end turn right, past the Coastguard Lookout to the Crab and Lobster. Walk across the pub car park towards the sea and at the top of the steps turn right along the footpath following the top of the coastal slope.

Cross the gravel car park and follow the coastal path for ¾ mile (1.2km) past open fields and through woodland until you emerge on to Bembridge School playing-fields. Continue to the far end of the playing-field and at this point, near the buildings, leave the coastal path by turning right along the public footpath with the flat-roofed building on your left. Join the school drive, then leave it by branching left by the 'Private' sign and follow the footpath through the trees to the road. Turn left down the hill and after 110yd (100m) turn right along the footpath by the camping site, passing into a wood. Cross the road and follow the footpath opposite through the wood. At the junction with the bridleway turn right up the hill to the windmill. Bembridge Windmill, built in 1746, was renovated in 1957 and handed to the National Trust. It is open to the public in the summer.

Continue ahead down the High Street then turn left opposite The Courtyard down the path signposted to Bembridge Point. Turn right at the bottom of the hill and follow the path through the woodland. This path follows part of the old harbour wall. The harbour used to extend inland as far as Brading and was reclaimed for agriculture in 1880. *Join the unmade road and follow it back to the car park.*

An early view of Bembridge from St Helens

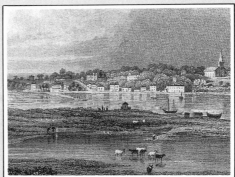

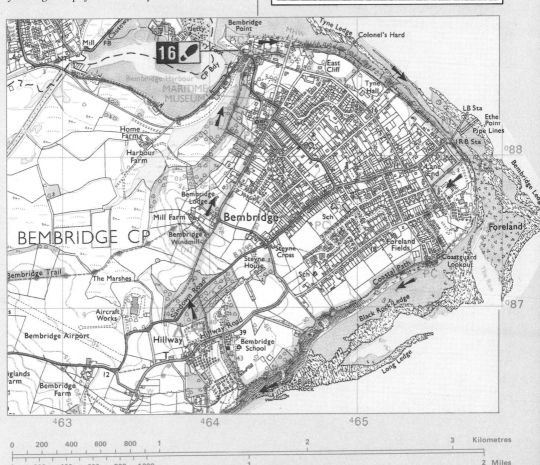

Index

Page numbers in bold type indicate main entries. See also Directory, page 73.

Acknowledgements

The publishers would like to thank the many individuals who helped in the preparation of this book. Special thanks are due to The Isle of Wight County Press, The Isle of Wight Ramblers' Association, The Isle of Wight Teachers' Centre and the Isle of Wight Tourist Board.

The Automobile Association also wishes to thank the following photographers, organisations and libraries for their assistance in the compilation of this book:

Bekens of Cowes 29 *Amandla Kulm*, 30/31 *Britannia* 1930, 31 *Velsheda* 1986, 31 *Velsheda* 1930, 32 *Tigre*, 76 *Jolie Brise*, 78 Admiral's Cup; *BBC Hulton Picture Library* 28 Mr & Mrs J B Priestley; *A R Cantwell* 12 Yarmouth Castle Cannon, 70 Fort Albert; *Carisbrooke Castle Museum* 10 Drawing of Carisbrooke Castle, 12/12 Early Map of Isle of Wight; *English Heritage* 42 Dining Room, Osborne House; *D Forss* 1 Ryde Pier; *O Frazer* 18 Wild Daffodil, 19 Pyramid Orchid, 21 Hoary Stock, 21 Adder, Great Green Bush Cricket; *A Goddard* 68 Vineyards; *Jessica Holm* 56 Red Squirrels; *A Insole* 17 Ladder Chine, 17 Hanover Point; *International Photobank* Front Cover Freshwater Bay; *The Isle of Wight Tourist Office* 53 River at Newport, 54 Newtown Old Town Hall; *R Johnson* 20/21 Tree Lupins, 69 Whippingham Church, Almshouses, Church Door, 76 Signpost, 77 Signpost, 92 Freshwater Church; *Mary Evans Picture Library* 26 Algernon Swinburne; *S & O Mathews* 3 Pond Green, 24 Blackgang Chine, 39 Carisbrooke Castle, 53 Newport, 101 Ventnor, 103 Appuldurcombe House, 104 Bonchurch, 109 Bembridge; *Nature Photographers* 55 Cormorant (P Carbo); *C R Pope* 63 Glanville Fritillary; *The Mansell Collection* 22/3 Wreck of the *Clarendon*, 27 Tennyson, 29 Cowes, 42/3 Osborne House, 49 Lewis Carroll, 49 Farringford; *D J Tonalin* 7 Chillerton Down Rampart, 8 Iron Age Gold Coin, 9 Anglo-Saxon Disc Brooch; *Woodmansterne Nicholas Servian* 34 Alum Bay, 60 Freshwater Bay.

The following photographs are from the Automobile Association's Photo Library:

S & O Mathews 5 Totland, 6 The Longstone, 8/9 Medina Mosaic, 9 Newport Roman Villa, 10/11 View of Carisbrooke Castle, 12 Yarmouth Castle & George Hotel, 13 Appuldurcombe House, 14/15 Headon Warren, 18 Parkhurst Forest, 22 St Catherine's Oratory, 25 Queen Victoria, 33 Ironwork at Cowes, 34 Coloured Sand, 34 Alverstoke, 35 Tennyson Monument, 36 Bembridge Windmill, 36 Bembridge Harbour, 37 Bembridge Maritime Museum, 37 Blackgang Chine, 38 Bonchurch Church, 38 Nunwell House at Brading, 39 Donkey Wheel, 40 Brighstone, 40 Brook, 41 Calbourne Farm House, 41 Winkle Street at Calbourne, 41 Carisbrooke Village, 42 Chale Green, 44 Cowes, 44 Cowes & Royal Yacht Squadron Cannons, 45 Fishbourne Ferry Terminal, 45 Fort Victoria, 45 Fishbourne, 46 Freshwater Bay, 47 St Agnes Church at Freshwater, 47 Golden Hill Fort, 48 Godshill Church & Cottages, 48 Godshill Model Village, 49 Gurnard, 50 Havenstreet Railway, 51 Landslip, 51 Mottistone Manor, 52 All Saints Church at Newchurch, 53 Newport Town Hall, 54 Newtown, 55 Bird Watcher, 56 Northwood Church, 57 Parkhurst Forest, 58 Robin Hill Park, 58 Deer, 59 Ryde High Street, 59 Hovercraft, 59 Ryde Pier, 60 Sileage Cutting, 61 Glass Blowing, 61 Tropical Bird Park, 62 Sandown, 63 Flamingo Park, 64 Shalfleet, 64 Shanklin, 65 The Old Chine, 65 Shanklin Shop, 65 Postcards, 66 Steephill Cove, 66 Totland Bay Notice, 66 Totland Bay, 68 Barton Manor Wines, 70 Wootton Creek, 72 Notice, 72 Yarmouth Harbour, 73 Brading Mosaic, 73 Arreton Craft Village, 75 Haseley Manor, 77 Walkers, 77 Notice, 79 The Needles; *W Voysey* 74 Newport Arts Centre; *H Williams* 71 Yafford Watermill.

Other Ordnance Survey Maps of the Isle of Wight

How to get there with Routemaster and Routeplanner Maps

Reach the Isle of Wight from Birmingham, Oxford, Guildford and London using Routemaster Sheet 9. Alternatively use the Ordnance Survey Great Britain Routeplanner map which covers the whole country on one sheet.

Exploring with Landranger, Tourist and Outdoor Leisure Maps

Landranger Series
1¼ inches to one mile or 1:50 000 scale

These maps cover the whole of Britain and are good for local motoring and walking.
Each contains tourist information such as parking, picnic places, viewpoints and rights of way.
The sheet covering the Isle of Wight is:

196 Solent & Isle of Wight

Tourist Map Series
1 inch to one mile or 1:63 360 scale

These maps cover popular holiday areas and are ideal for discovering the countryside. In addition to normal map detail, ancient monuments, camping and caravanning sites, parking facilities and viewpoints are marked. Lists of selected places of interest are included on some sheets and others include useful guides to the area.

Tourist Map Sheet 6 covers part of the Isle of Wight.

Outdoor Leisure Map Series
2½ inches to one mile or 1:25 000 scale

These maps cover popular leisure and recreation areas of the country and include details of Youth Hostels, camping and caravanning sites, picnic areas, footpaths and viewpoints.

Outdoor Leisure Map Sheet 29 covers the Isle of Wight.

Other titles available in this series are:

Channel Islands
Cornwall
Cotswolds
Devon
Forest of Dean & Wye Valley

Ireland
Lake District
New Forest
Northumbria
North Yorkshire Moors

Peak District
Scottish Highlands
South Downs
Wessex
Yorkshire Dales